麦格希 中英双语阅读文库

# 世界未解之谜

【美】富尔顿(Fulton, L.) ●主编
刘慧 ●译
麦格希中英双语阅读文库编委会 ●编

全国百佳图书出版单位
吉林出版集团股份有限公司

## 图书在版编目（CIP）数据

世界未解之谜 / (美) 富尔顿 (Fulton, L.) 主编；刘慧译；麦格希中英双语阅读文库编委会编. -- 2版. -- 长春：吉林出版集团股份有限公司，2018.3（2022.1重印）
（麦格希中英双语阅读文库）
ISBN 978-7-5581-4784-5

Ⅰ.①世… Ⅱ.①富… ②刘… ③麦… Ⅲ.①英语—汉语—对照读物②科学知识—普及读物 Ⅳ.
①H319.4：Z

中国版本图书馆CIP数据核字(2018)第046066号

### 世界未解之谜

编：麦格希中英双语阅读文库编委会
插　　画：齐　航　李延霞
责任编辑：王芳芳
封面设计：冯冯翼
开　　本：660mm×960mm　1/16
字　　数：176千字
印　　张：10
版　　次：2018年3月第2版
印　　次：2022年1月第2次印刷

出　　版：吉林出版集团股份有限公司
发　　行：吉林出版集团外语教育有限公司
地　　址：长春市福祉大路5788号龙腾国际大厦B座7层
　　　　　邮编：130011
电　　话：总编办：0431-81629929
　　　　　发行部：0431-81629927　0431-81629921(Fax)
印　　刷：北京一鑫印务有限责任公司

ISBN 978-7-5581-4784-5　　　定价：36.00元
版权所有　　侵权必究　　举报电话：0431-81629929

# 前言 PREFACE

英国思想家培根说过：阅读使人深刻。阅读的真正目的是获取信息，开拓视野和陶冶情操。从语言学习的角度来说，学习语言若没有大量阅读就如隔靴搔痒，因为阅读中的语言是最丰富、最灵活、最具表现力、最符合生活情景的，同时读物中的情节、故事引人入胜，进而能充分调动读者的阅读兴趣，培养读者的文学修养，至此，语言的学习水到渠成。

"麦格希中英双语阅读文库"在世界范围内选材，涉及科普、社会文化、文学名著、传奇故事、成长励志等多个系列，充分满足英语学习者课外阅读之所需，在阅读中学习英语、提高能力。

◎难度适中

本套图书充分照顾读者的英语学习阶段和水平，从读者的阅读兴趣出发，以难易适中的英语语言为立足点，选材精心、编排合理。

◎精品荟萃

本套图书注重经典阅读与实用阅读并举。既包含国内外脍炙人口、耳熟能详的美文，又包含科普、人文、故事、励志类等多学科的精彩文章。

◎功能实用

本套图书充分体现了双语阅读的功能和优势，充分考虑到读者课外阅读的方便，超出核心词表的词汇均出现在使其意义明显的语境之中，并标注释义。

鉴于编者水平有限，凡不周之处，谬误之处，皆欢迎批评教正。

我们真心地希望本套图书承载的文化知识和英语阅读的策略对提高读者的英语著作欣赏水平和英语运用能力有所裨益。

丛书编委会

# Contents

**T**otem Poles
图腾柱 / 1

Searching for the Loch Ness Monster
寻找尼斯湖水怪 / 11

What the Boys Found
男孩们发现了什么 / 25

Mysteries of the Lost Civilization
消失的文明之谜 / 40

Mummies
木乃伊 / 55

Early Birds: Fossils and Feathers
早期鸟类：化石和羽毛 / 72

**B**elieve It or Not?
信不信由你 / 86

The Mystery of King Tut
图坦王之谜 / 105

Prehistoric Giants
史前巨型动物 / 130

◆ TOTEM POLES

# Totem Poles

### Monuments of Cedar

Carving a bird from a block of wood is hard work, but imagine carving animals on a piece of wood as long as a tree trunk! Native peoples living along the Pacific coast of Alaska and Canada have been doing just that for hundreds of years. These carvings are called *totem* poles.

### Totem Poles Speak

Totem poles are carved in different *styles* and for different

---

# 图腾柱

### 雪松的纪念碑

用一块木头刻一只鸟是一件很不容易的事情，你可以想象一下在树干一样长的木头上刻动物该有多么不容易！生活在阿拉斯加和加拿大地区，太平洋沿岸的土著人做这种东西已经有几百年的历史了。这些雕刻的东西叫作图腾柱。

### 图腾柱会讲话

图腾柱有不同的雕刻的风格，也有不同的雕刻目的。柱子上刻下的图

---

monument *n.* 纪念碑　　　　　　　　　　　　totem *n.* 图腾
style *n.* 风格

**WORLD MYSTERIES**

◆ TOTEM POLES

reasons. The figures carved on the poles have special meanings and help tell stories. *Memorial* poles describe someone's life or a special event. Other totem poles tell the history of a *clan*, or family group, and still others welcome visitors.

  Many houses have totem poles that are part of the house itself. House poles are carved into the doorways, on the outside corners, or on poles that support the roof. These poles show the wealth and *status* of the family.

---

形有着特殊的意义，让我想到其后面的故事。纪念柱子介绍某个人的生平或者是某个事件。还有的柱子讲述某个氏族或家族的历史，还有的柱子是对访客的欢迎。

  很多房子前都有图腾柱，这也是房子本身的一个部分。图腾柱被雕刻在门廊内、墙角的外面，或者是房顶的支柱上。这些柱子代表着这个家庭的财富和地位。

---

memorial *adj.* 纪念性的        clan *n.* 宗族；氏族
status *n.* 社会地位

## WORLD MYSTERIES

*Mortuary* poles are like *gravestones*. The carvings on the pole honor the life of a person who has died. They tell about important events and family relationships in the dead person's life.

Some totem poles welcome visitors to a village. These are typically single human figures. They are put near a beach to show visitors that they are welcome.

One totem pole tells the legend of how Killer Whale clan took Black Bear for its *crest*, or special symbol.

One day, a hunter went into the mountains looking for mountain

---

　　太平间的柱子很像墓碑，柱子上的雕刻用来纪念死者的生活，讲述死者一生中的重要事件和家庭关系。
　　一些图腾柱是用来欢迎客人的。一般都是一个人的形象，常被放在海滨，表示对客人的欢迎。
　　一个图腾柱讲述了凯勒维尔氏族的传说，说明为什么他们用黑熊作为家族饰章或特殊标志。
　　一天，一个猎人走进了山林，寻找山羊。黑熊抓住了他，把他带到了

---

mortuary *n.* 太平间　　　　　　　　　　　　　　gravestone *n.* 墓碑
crest *n.* 饰章

◆ TOTEM POLES

goats. Black Bear captured him and brought the hunter to his *den*. The man lived with Black Bear. Although they became friends, the man missed his village.

After two years, Black Bear let the man go home. By now, the man looked like a bear. The villagers ran from him. Finally, one kind man *rubbed* medicine on the man's body. Soon the man looked human again, and he took Black Bear as his crest. His friend, Black Bear, always protected the man's family.

These illustrations show some of the most common figures you can see on totem poles.

Raven: Bird with a straight *beak*.

Raven is a *trickster* who can change shape into almost everything—a bird, a human, or even a speck of dirt.

---

自己的洞穴里，猎人与黑熊一起生活。尽管他们成了朋友，但是猎人非常想念自己的村庄。

两年以后，黑熊同意猎人回家，此时的猎人已经很像熊了。村民见他就跑，最后有一个善良的人在他的身上涂了药物，于是他又恢复了人的样子，后来他把黑熊作为他的饰章。他的这个黑熊朋友，总会保护这个猎人的家人。

下面这些是图腾柱中最常见的图案。

渡鸦：一种喙很直的鸟。

渡鸦是一种可以变成各用形状的骗子，可以变成鸟、人，或者还可以变成一个污点。

---

den *n.* 兽穴
beak *n.* 喙

rub *v.* 擦
trickster *n.* 骗子

## WORLD MYSTERIES

Bear: Round ears, many teeth.

Bear is a caring, good-like creature that can change from bear to human form.

*Beaver*: Long front teeth, *flat* tail with *crisscross* lines.

Beaver is a clever carver whose powerful tail-slap can cause earthquakes or turn him invisible.

Watchmen: Crouching men with very tall hats.

Watchmen are human figures who can spot danger from far away.

Thunderbird: Curly feathers that look like *horns*.

Thunderbird is one of the Native Americans' most powerful spirits. He causes thunder and lightning, and is large enough to

---

熊：圆耳朵，很多牙齿。

熊是一种充满爱心，形象好看的动物，可以由熊变成人形。

海狸：前牙很长，扁平的尾巴，上面有十字线条。

海狸是精明的雕刻师，他用尾巴敲击的力量能够引起地震，或者让自己不被看见。

看门人：蹲坐着的人，戴着高高的帽子。

看门人是人的形象，可以看到远处的危险。

雷鸟：羽毛卷曲，看起来有些像动物的角。

雷鸟是土著美洲人最有威力的精灵，他能引发雷声和闪电。并且大到

---

beaver *n.* 海狸　　　　　　　　　　　　　　　　　　flat *adj.* 平的
crisscross *adj.* 十字交叉的　　　　　　　　　　　　horn *n.* 角

◆ TOTEM POLES

## WORLD MYSTERIES

catch a whale in his *talons*.

Wolf: Pointed ears, long *snout*, many sharp teeth.

Wolf is not friendly to humans, though it knows the secrets of healing.

### Carving a Totem Pole

In the past, a clan would hire a master carver to make a totem pole. Today, many museums, businesses, and people around the world also want totem poles created for them. First, they hire a carver and work with him or her to plan the pole.

The carver finds a tree with no *knots* or bends. The carver cuts down the tree, cuts off the branches, and *hauls* it to the workshop. Then the carver chips away the soft outer wood.

---

可以用爪子抓住鲸鱼。

狼：耳朵尖、鼻子长，有很多锋利的牙齿。

狼与人类不友好，但它们知道治病的秘诀。

雕刻图腾柱

过去的氏族会雇用雕刻大师来刻图腾柱。现在世界上很多博物馆、企业和个人都需要为自己雕刻图腾柱。他们先雇用一个雕刻师，让雕刻师为他们设计这个柱子。

雕刻师先要找一棵没有节没有弯的树，把树砍下来，去掉树枝，把它拖到工作室。然后雕刻师除去树表层的松软层。

---

talon *n.* 爪      snout *n.* 鼻子
knot *n.* 节子；结疤      haul *v.* （用力地）拉

◆ TOTEM POLES

Often, a team of carvers works on the totem pole. The master carver draws the *designs* on the log with *charcoal*. The master carver works on the bottom figure of the pole because this figure is the biggest and most important, and everyone can see it up close. Helpers carve and paint other figures on the totem pole. Carving a big pole can take as long as nine months.

When the pole is ready, it is brought to the place where it will stand. A potlatch is held to *celebrate* the raising of the pole. There is *feasting*, dancing, singing, and gift giving, and the totem pole's stories are told. Prayers and blessings may be said for the pole and for the people who own it.

---

通常是多个雕刻匠共同刻一个图腾柱。雕刻大师用碳笔在圆木上画出图案，雕刻大师负责雕刻柱子的最下面的部分，因为这部分最大也最重要，而且人们看得也比较仔细。助手们负责柱子的其他部分。雕刻一个大的柱子有时需要九个月的时间。

柱子刻好后，被运送到竖立的地点。人们在这里举行一个冬节庆祝竖立柱子。人们享用美食、跳舞、唱歌、送礼物，讲述图腾柱的故事，还会为柱子及柱子的主人祈祷和祝福。

---

design *n.* 设计  
celebrate *v.* 庆祝  
charcoal *n.* 木炭  
feast *v.* 尽情享用（美味佳肴）

**WORLD MYSTERIES**

**Totem Poles Come Home**

When European *explorers* came to the coast of Alaska and Canada in the 1800s, they were *impressed* by the many totem poles they found. Many of the poles were taken away and ended up in museums.

In 1990, the U.S. passed a law that said native peoples would be able to get back *property* that had been taken from them. Because of this law, many totem poles are returning to their original homes and to the people who created them.

---

图腾柱回家

19世纪欧洲探险家来到了阿拉斯加和加拿大的海岸线上，他们对见到的很多图腾柱印象深刻。他们带走了很多的图腾柱，并放在博物馆里。

1990年，美国通过法律，土著人可以取回被别人拿走的财产。因为这项法律，很多图腾柱回到了它们的家，回到了雕刻它们的人们那里。

---

explorer *n.* 探险者  　　　　　　　　　　impress *v.* 给……以深刻印象
property *n.* 财产

# 2

# Searching for the Loch Ness Monster

**The Loch**

Skye and Ross thought they were too old to look for *fabled* monsters in the British Isles. They just wanted to stay in their hotel room and play with their PSPs. But like much of their trip to Scotland, they had to go along for the ride. As they drove through green *glens* dotted with sheep, Ross asked from the *backseat*, "So what's a loch, anyway?"

Their mom said, "It sounds like a door lock that keeps people

---

## 寻找尼斯湖水怪

**尼斯湖**

斯凯和罗斯觉得去不列颠群岛寻找传说中的怪物是小孩子做的事情。他们只想待在旅馆房间，玩玩游戏机就好了。全家人之前到苏格兰的旅行都是自驾出游，这次也是一样。他们开车经过翠绿的峡谷，看见一些绵羊，罗斯坐在后座上问道："到底loch（湖）是什么呢？"

妈妈说："loch（湖）这个词和把人锁在屋外的lock（锁）听起来很

---

fabled  *adj.* 传说中的  
backseat  *n.* 后座

glen  *n.* 峡谷

**WORLD MYSTERIES**

◆ SEARCHING FOR THE LOCH NESS MONSTER

out of a house. But this loch is a lake that invites people in. People don't want to swim in it because it's so cold, but it *invites* people's imaginations to play."

Their dad added, "Loch is the word used in Scotland for 'lake', and Ness is the name of this lake. Scotland has many other lochs, but Loch Ness has the most water. In fact, Loch Ness is the largest fresh water lake in the British Isles."

"How big is it?" asked Skye as they drove along the *shore*. "It sure isn't very wide like the lakes at home in Wisconsin."

"It looks more like a river than a lake." Ross chimed in as he stared at the loch through the car window.

"Let's stop at this information center." their mom *suggested*. "We'll

---

像。但这个尼斯湖却是请人进来。湖水太凉，人们不想在湖里面游泳，但在人们可以发挥想象力来玩乐。"

爸爸又说："在苏格兰语里，loch(湖)就是英文中的lake(湖)，这个湖的名字叫尼斯。苏格兰还有很多其他的湖，但尼斯湖的水量是最多的。其实，尼斯湖是不列颠群岛中最大的淡水湖。"

"这个湖有多大？"当车沿海岸开过时，斯凯问道。"它肯定没有我们家乡威斯康星州的湖那么宽。"

"这看起来更像河，不像湖。"罗斯边看着车窗外的湖边插话说。

"我们就在信息中心这停车吧，"妈妈建议说。"在这可以多了解一

---

invite *v.* 邀请  shore *n.* 岸
suggest *v.* 建议

## WORLD MYSTERIES

learn more about it."

Inside the center were *displays*, signs, and *brochures* to look at and read. They learned that Loch Ness was formed during the last ice age. In the same period, North America was created, Britain pulled away from Europe's mainland, and Scotland split in two. Earthquakes made a trench that glaciers covered until about 12,000 years ago. When the ice melted, it filled the trench with water to form the loch.

### The Legend

"I guess it's possible that people are seeing a real creature," sighed Skye. "But I think it's just the dark *ripples* of the water."

"Who knows, maybe the Loch Ness Monster will be described

---

些尼斯湖的情况。"

  信息中心里是供游客观看的展品、标志和供阅读的小册子的地方。全家人知道了尼斯湖是在上一个冰河时代形成的。在同一时期，北美洲诞生，英国从欧洲大陆上分离出来，苏格兰被一分为二。地震形成了一条深沟被冰川覆盖，这一切发生在大约12,000年前。冰川融化后，冰水流入深沟形成了尼斯湖。

  传说

  斯凯叹气道："我猜很有可能人们看到的是一个大生物，但我认为它只是湖水泛起的暗色的微波。"

  他们的妈妈说道："谁知道呢，可能尼斯湖怪物有一天会成为鱼的新

---

display *n.* 陈列；展出      brochure *n.* 小册子
ripple *n.* 涟漪

### SEARCHING FOR THE LOCH NESS MONSTER

one day as a new species of fish that is no longer a mystery," added their mom. "But maybe the greatest appeal of the Loch Ness Monster is that it is a mystery. For now, the legend continues to capture people's imaginations."

A map showed that Loch Ness is 24 miles (39 km) long, 1 mile (1.6 km) wide, and over 800 feet (244 m) deep in some places—much deeper than the seas around the British Isles.

"Check this out," Skye said, reading from an information *panel* near the map. "Peat, a *layer* of dead plant material, is so thick in the water that light only travels as deep as a few yards. As a result, sunlight can't warm the loch, so it's too cold for people to swim in."

Ross picked up where Skye left off. "The top 100 feet, or 30.5 meters, warm up to 54 degrees Fahrenheit in summer. That's 12 degrees Celsius. The rest stays at 42 degrees Fahrenheit, or 6

---

物种，而不再是个谜。但可能尼斯湖最大的吸引力就是它的怪物。从现在开始，传说继续开发人们的想象力。"

地图上显示，尼斯湖长24英里（39千米），宽1英里（1.6千米），部分湖区深达800英尺（244米）——这一深度要比不列颠群岛周围的海都深得多。

"快看这，"斯凯说。她在地图旁边的信息板上读到"泥煤是由死去的植物构成的，泥煤层过厚，光线在水中只能穿过几码的深度。所以，阳光不能进入湖中使湖水升温，导致湖水过于冰冷，人们无法在湖中游泳。"

罗斯接着读了下去。"最上面的100英尺湖水（30.5米），在夏季温度最高为54华氏度，也就是12摄氏度。全年其余时候，湖水温度为42华

---

panel  n.  壁板　　　　　　　　　　　　　　　　　　layer  n.  层

**WORLD MYSTERIES**

degrees Celsius, year round. Because of this, most life in the loch, such as fish and seals, stays close to the surface."

"Look here," their dad said. "Guided boat rides are available on Loch Ness for fun, or you can search for the Loch Ness Monster with sonar."

"Maybe we could *windsurf* or water-ski on the loch," Ross said, thinking that sounded like more fun than a boat ride. "But we would need special cold-water equipment, and it says here that people usually do those activities only on the weekends."

"They don't want to *disturb* Nessie, the monster," joked Skye, as she pointed to the last information panel.

"Yeah, right," Ross *snorted*. "As if anyone would take a legend seriously!"

---

氏度，也就是6摄氏度。因此，尼斯湖中的大部分生物，像鱼和海豹，都生活在接近水面的地方。"

"看这里，"爸爸说。"尼斯湖有带导游的船供娱乐，你也可以用声呐去寻找尼斯湖水怪。"

罗斯说："也许我们可以在湖上冲浪或滑水。"他觉得这听起来比划船有趣多了。"但是我们需要特殊的冷水装备，这里写着人们通常只在周末才有这些活动。"

斯凯指着最后一块信息板，开玩笑说："他们不想打扰水怪。"

罗斯不屑地说："是，对啊，就好像谁能把那些传说当真似的！"

---

windsurf *v.* 风帆冲浪　　　　　　　　　　　　disturb *v.* 打扰
snort *v.* 喷鼻息；哼

◆ SEARCHING FOR THE LOCH NESS MONSTER

## WORLD MYSTERIES

"Let's take a boat ride and hear what the local expert has to say about it," said their dad.

### The Monster

On the boat, their guide said, in her Scottish *brogue*, "Welcome, lads and lassies, to your private showing of the Loch Ness Monster's *lair*.

"For over 1,400 years, people have taken Nessie sightings seriously. Scientists have even used NASA's computers, along with underwater cameras and other equipment, to test the loch. But long before this testing began in the 1970s, other reliable sources caught *glimpses* of the 'monster' in the loch."

"The first recorded sighting was in AD 565, when an Irish

---

"我们乘船过去，听听当地的专家怎么说吧，"爸爸说。

水怪

在船上，他们的导游带着浓重的苏格兰口音讲到，"女士们先生们，欢迎各位来此参观尼斯湖水怪的藏身之处。"

"1400多年来，人们对水怪的存在深信不疑。科学家们甚至运用了美国国家航空航天局的电脑，加上水下照相机和其他的设备，来到尼斯湖做测试。这项测试开始于20世纪70年代，此前，已有其他可靠消息称曾瞥见过湖里的'怪物'。"

"有记载的第一次亲眼见证尼斯湖水怪是在公元565年，有个叫作

---

brogue *n.* 口音      lair *n.* 兽穴；兽窝
glimpse *n.* 一瞥；一看

### ◆ SEARCHING FOR THE LOCH NESS MONSTER

*missionary* named Saint Columba asked his servant to swim across the loch to get a boat. A creature came to the surface, roared, and opened its mouth. Columba commanded it to go back, be quiet, and not touch the man. The monster obeyed, and every sighting since then has been quiet and peaceful.

"People were relatively quiet about Nessie sightings until the 1930s, when cameras became popular. That's when interest in Nessie hunting took off in a flash. *Monks* at the *monastery* on the banks of the loch reported seeing Nessie's submarine-shaped back and long neck. Thousands of highlanders have signed a statement promising that they've seen the monster. Most sightings have occurred near the ruins of Urquhart Castle, halfway up the loch.

---

圣·科伦巴的爱尔兰传教士让他的仆人游过尼斯湖去叫船。只见有一个怪物冲出水面，大声咆哮，并且张开大嘴。科伦巴命令怪物退回去，安静下来，不准碰那个仆人。怪物乖乖听话，此后每一次与怪物的见面都安静、平和。"

"在20世纪30年代以前，人们对于见到水怪的消息反应相对平静。但此后，随着照相机的普及，人们要捕捉水怪的热情暴涨，一发而不可收。住在湖边寺庙里的僧侣们说看见了水怪像潜水艇形状的背部和长长的脖子。有数千名住在苏格兰高地的人签署了声明，认定自己见过水怪。大部分人说是在湖的上游，也就是在厄克特城堡废墟附近见到水怪出没的。"

---

missionary *n.* 传教士　　　　　　　　　　　　　　monk *n.* 僧侣
monastery *n.* 寺院

**WORLD MYSTERIES**

"These monster sightings are not unique to Loch Ness. People have reported seeing similar creatures in at least 265 lakes and rivers around the world. Some people think these creatures must be a type of water mammal or fish, such as a seal or giant *sturgeon*."

"Some think the Nessie sightings are of a prehistoric reptile that somehow survived over millions of years. They say that when the trench was created during the last ice age, a prehistoric beast or group of beasts was left behind in the *upheaval* and became landlocked."

"Some accept the reports of Nessie as fact. Others think of the reports as legends created to keep children away from the deep, cold waters of the loch."

"That would keep you away," *teased* Skye as she *nudged* Ross in

---

"有人见到水怪的情况不是尼斯湖独有的。在全世界至少256个湖泊中，有人声称看到过类似水怪的生物。有人认为这些生物只是某种生活在水中的哺乳动物或鱼类，比如说海豹或一条大鲟鱼。"

"有人认为所见到的水怪其实是史前爬行动物，但已经活了几百万年。他们说当年冰河时代形成深沟的时候，有一只或若干只史前动物在剧变中掉队，变成了内陆水域动物。"

"有人相信关于水怪的报道是真实的。还有人则认为水怪的传说是人们编造出来的，好让小孩子远离深邃冰冷的湖水。"

斯凯逗罗斯说："就是让你离得远点，"边说边推了推罗斯。罗斯就

---

sturgeon *n.* 鲟鱼  
tease *v.* 戏弄；寻开心

upheaval *n.* 剧变  
nudge *v.* 轻推

◆ SEARCHING FOR THE LOCH NESS MONSTER

the ribs. He looked at her with crossed eyes and a scrunched-up nose.

The tour guide continued, "People eager to put the legend to rest or prove the monster's existence have *scoured* the loch for Nessie. Scientists got involved because there was enough consistent evidence that people couldn't explain. For example, sonar picked up a long moving object 480 feet down, which is too deep for any known modern fish. In 1987, scientists launched 'Operation Deep Scan,' using 24 boats to map the loch with sonar *equipment*."

"What did they find?" asked Ross, not realizing he was getting interested.

---

用斗鸡眼看着斯凯，还皱着鼻子。

　　导游继续说道："想要推翻这个传说的人和想要证明有水怪的人都来到尼斯湖一探真相。科学家也参与其中，因为不断有充分证据表明出现了人们无法解释的事情。比如说，声波定位仪曾经在480英尺的水下发现长条的移动物体，而任何已知的现代鱼类都不可能在这么深的位置生存。1987年，科学家们发起了'深水扫描行动'，使用24艘装有声波定位仪的船只搜寻整个尼斯湖。"

　　"他们发现什么了？"罗斯问道。他还没意识到自己已经对水怪的故事感兴趣了。

---

scour *v.* 四处搜索　　　　　　　equipment *n.* 设备；装备

## WORLD MYSTERIES

"They could explain some sounds as echoes from the loch's *steep* sides. But they could not explain at least one echo from a 'large and moving' object 200 feet down."

"Beep, beep, beep, beep." The sonar on the boat had found something. The passengers all crowded to the screen to see the image as the boat passed over something. But it was only a log. *Disappointed*, they sat back down and the tour guide continued.

"Studying the loch has turned up other findings. In 1981, the Loch Ness Project found fish called red-bellied Arctic char. They had been living in the waters at 700 feet deep for over 12,000 years—since the last ice age."

"他们将一些声音解释为尼斯湖陡峭的湖岸产生的回音。但对于来自200英尺深水的'巨大的移动的'物体发出的声音，科学家们也无法解释。"

"嘀，嘀，嘀，嘀。"船上的声波定位仪搜寻到了什么。所有乘客都挤到屏幕前一看究竟，结果却只是一根原木。乘客们非常失望，坐回原位听导游继续讲。

"对尼斯湖的探索还带来了其他收获。1981年，'尼斯湖项目'发现了一种叫做'寒水鲑鱼'的红肚子鱼。在上个冰河世纪后的12,000年里，这种鱼一直生活在700英尺的深水下。"

steep *adj.* 陡峭的　　　　　　　disappointed *adj.* 失望的

◆ SEARCHING FOR THE LOCH NESS MONSTER

"Experts had thought the waters were too cold for life below a few hundred feet, so this discovery surprised them. They also think the waters are too cold for *reptiles*, which would *debunk* one theory that the monster is a *plesiosaur*. But they're still learning about the age of dinosaurs and now think that some dinosaurs were warm-blooded. If the monster were warm-blooded, it might have been able to survive in the cold waters of the loch."

"Wow!" exclaimed their dad. "So whether they find the monster or not, their studies of the loch have been valuable."

The boat reached the dock, and it was time for them to *disembark*.

"专家们认为100英尺以下的湖水对于生物来讲过于寒冷，所以这样的发现使他们大吃一惊。他们认为尼斯湖水对于爬行动物来说也过于寒冷，所以驳倒了这水怪可能是蛇颈龙的说法。但他们仍然在研究一些恐龙的年龄，现在认为有些恐龙属于热血动物。如果水怪是热血的，它就可能在尼斯湖的冷水中存活下来。"

"哇！"爸爸惊叹道。"所以，无论他们有没有找到水怪，这些对于尼斯湖的研究都非常有价值。"

船到了码头，人们该下船了。

reptile *n.* 爬行动物　　　　　　　　　　　debunk *v.* 揭穿
plesiosaur *n.* 蛇颈龙　　　　　　　　　　 disembark *v.* 登陆

## WORLD MYSTERIES

### A Sighting?

After lunch, Skye and Ross *skipped* rocks in the loch, doubtful they would spot Nessie's curved black *hump*. They heard their parents tossing around theories about the monster, as if it were a mystery they could solve in an afternoon. But standing on the *grassy* banks of the loch, Ross was sure he spotted Nessie's tail dipping back into the black water ...

---

眼见为实？

午饭后，斯凯和罗斯在湖面玩跳石头，心想会不会看到水怪背部的深色突起。他们听见父母亲还在争论有关水怪的说法，好像他们一个下午就能把这个谜解开似的。但罗斯站在尼斯湖长满草的岸边时，他确定自己看见了水怪的尾巴钻进黑黑的湖水中去了……

---

skip　*v.*　蹦跳　　　　　　　　　　　　　　　　　　　　hump　*n.*　隆起物
grassy　*adj.*　长满草的

# 3

♦ WHAT THE BOYS FOUND

# What the Boys Found

**Discovery in the Woods**

Have you ever been out for a walk and *stumbled* over a mysterious hole? Did you *hesitate*, look down into the darkness, and wonder what was under there? Well, that's just what happened to four teenage boys near Lascaux manor in southern France on a warm September day in 1940.

Marcel Ravidat, three friends, and a dog were exploring the woods around the town of Montignac, when they discovered the hole. Several years before, a large pine tree had been struck by

---

## 男孩们发现了什么

树林里的发现

你有没有在散步途中误闯进一个神秘的洞穴？你是不是犹豫着，在黑暗中四下张望，很奇怪里面到底有些什么？嗯，这就是1940年9月很温暖的一天，在法国南部拉斯科庄园附近发生在四个男孩子身上的故事。

马塞尔·哈维达和他的三个朋友还有一条狗在蒙特涅克镇的树林里探险时，发现了一个洞穴。几年以前，一棵大松树受雷击倒地。形成一个宽

---

stumble v. 跟跄；绊脚                    hesitate v. 犹豫；迟疑

## WORLD MYSTERIES

lightning and tumbled over, exposing a gaping entrance to what turned out to be one of history's most interesting treasures.

As the dog barked excitedly, Marcel and his friends dropped to their knees and peered into the hole. Without a light it was impossible to make out what lay below, but they could tell that something hollow and thrilling was hidden there. They had a feeling that the opening was something other than a *burrow* or a tunnel created by a mole or a *groundhog*.

The boys could barely contain their excitement. What had they found? Was this a cave, or perhaps a long-buried tomb? They felt they had to follow their *instincts* and continue their exploration. They made plans to return with a light and some *shovels*.

---

宽的裂口，通往到被后人认为是有史以来最有趣的宝藏。

　　狗开始狂叫，马歇尔和他的朋友们俯身在地，向洞里面瞄进去。没有光亮，看不出里面都有什么。但孩子们确定里面很空旷、藏着很刺激的东西。他们感觉到这处裂口绝不是鼹鼠或土拨鼠挖出来的地洞或地道那么简单。

　　几个男孩子难以抑制自己的激动心情。他们发现了什么？这是一处洞穴，还是埋藏已久的墓穴呢？他们感到应当跟随直觉，继续探索。于是计划回去带来光源，再找几把铲子。

---

burrow *n.* 洞穴　　　　　　　　　　　　groundhog *n.* 土拨鼠
instinct *n.* 直觉　　　　　　　　　　　　shovel *n.* 铲

◆ WHAT THE BOYS FOUND

WORLD MYSTERIES

**Exploring the Cave**

A few days later, Marcel and his friends returned to the hole with a lantern. Digging quickly, they enlarged the hole, and one by one they slipped into it, fell onto a pile of rocks, and looked around. Their light was very dim, and it took several minutes to become *accustomed* to the darkness in this underground space.

They saw that another entrance, almost a doorway into a shadowy space beyond, was behind some rocks. They looked at each other, nodded and *shrugged*, then held the lantern higher and moved into a large, dark space.

The boys continued to explore the cave together, going deeper and deeper into the ground until they *encountered* a deep, narrow

---

洞穴内的探索

过了几天，马塞尔和他的朋友们带着灯笼回到了洞穴。他们很快挖大洞口，一个接一个地钻进去，落脚在一堆石头上，四下看起来。光线很弱，但几分钟后几个人就适应了这里的昏暗。

他们看到在一些岩石后有另外一个入口，从那可以进入到前面一处比较暗的地方。他们对视了一下，彼此点头、耸肩示意，举高灯笼，进入了一个很宽敞的暗处。

男孩子们继续探索洞穴，越走越深，一直走到一处低洼、狭窄的通

---

accustomed *adj.* 习惯于　　　　　　　　　　　　　　shrug *v.* 耸肩
encounter *v.* 遭遇

◆ WHAT THE BOYS FOUND

passage too small for all of them to get through. After talking it over, they decided that Marcel should go forward alone. He would take the lantern and enlarge the passageway, then return for the others.

Carrying the lantern, a shovel, and some rope, Marcel *squeezed* through the space, digging as he went. After a while he lowered the rope and dropped down a shaft into a *cavernous* room below.

Holding the lantern higher, he *peered* through the darkness at the walls surrounding him. The walls were covered with bas-relief (images that are carved out of a surface making the image raised from the surface) paintings of animals.

Marcel moved closer. Images of horses, cows, stags, and bison seemed to dance and *gallop* and swim across the walls of the cave.

---

道，他们中有的人进不去。商量之后，他们决定让马塞尔独自前行。大家商量好让他提着灯笼拓宽通道，然后再回来让其他人通过。

马塞尔提着灯笼，带着一把铲子和一些绳索，挤进了那条窄道，边走边挖。过了一会，就把绳子吊下去，顺着绳子进入下面的穴室。

马塞尔举高灯笼，在黑暗中努力看清四周的墙壁。墙上画满了动物的浮雕（即在墙壁表面作画使所画形象从墙表突出）。

他又靠近了一些。洞穴的墙壁上，画有马匹、母牛、驯鹿和野牛，或奔腾，或疾驰，或游弋，千姿百态。

---

squeeze v. 挤进
peer v. 费力地看

cavernous adj. 像洞穴的
gallop v. 疾驰

## WORLD MYSTERIES

Marcel could barely contain himself. He hurried out of the room and climbed up. As he made his way back to his friends, he noticed other pictures on the walls of the passageway.

### More Questions, More Exploration

By the next morning, the news of the boys' discovery had spread throughout the village. Villagers *descended* upon the cave and found other rooms filled with new and exciting carvings. Clearly, these works of art were very, very old, and before long *archaeologists* came to the cave to study them.

Archaeologists are scientists who study *ancient* cultures using the objects that people leave behind. The archaeologists looked at the pictures very carefully, and the longer they looked the more questions they asked.

---

马塞尔感觉难以置信。他匆忙出了穴室，向上爬。他想回去见他的朋友，回去的路上却在通道的墙壁上发现了更多的图画。

问题越多，探索越深

到第二天早晨，孩子们发现洞穴的消息传遍了整个村庄。村民们蜂拥而至，发现了更多的"房间"，墙壁上也都是新奇刺激的雕刻。很明显，这些作品有着极其悠久的历史，不久以后考古学家们就来到洞穴进行研究。

考古学家是通过研究古人留下的东西来钻研古代文化的科学家。考古学家们非常仔细地观察这些图画，观察得越久，产生的问题就越多。

---

descend *v.* 下；下来 　　　　　　　archaeologist *n.* 考古学家
ancient *adj.* 古代的

◆ WHAT THE BOYS FOUND

Who painted these *mysterious* paintings, and how old were they? Why were they painted in underground caves? Why did the artists paint only large birds and animals, like horses and bulls, and ignore small creatures such as snakes and fish? How could such perfect art be created in such a dark space? There were tiny holes in the wall halfway up to the high ceiling. Why? What purpose did they serve?

These paintings were clearly very old. But how old? The archaeologists began by trying to figure out when the paintings were created. To do so they tried several different methods.

Many scientists started by looking at the paintings themselves. They *analyzed* the dyes, paints, or other materials used to create colors. If the artists used *charcoal*, scientists might be able to date

---

是谁创作这些神秘的画作，他们有多大年纪了？他们为什么在地下洞穴作画？为什么他们所画的只有大鸟和马、牛一类的动物，却没有其他的小生物，比如蛇或鱼？在这样昏暗的环境下怎能创作出如此完美的艺术作品？在通往洞穴顶的墙壁上半部有一些小孔。为什么？这些孔是做什么的？

很明显，这些画有着悠久的历史。但有多悠久？考古学家们开始试图研究出画作的创作时间。为此，他们使用了几种方法。

许多科学家先是看壁画本身。他们分析染料、颜料以及着色时所用的其他材料。如果作者用过炭笔，科学家们就可以使用放射性碳方法追溯其

---

mysterious *adj.* 神秘的  analyze *v.* 分析
charcoal *n.* 木炭

## WORLD MYSTERIES

them using the *radiocarbon* method (things that contain carbon can be dated by measuring how much the carbon has changed). But they found that these pictures could not be dated in this way.

The scientists had to lower their eyes to find the answers to their questions. On the ground, below the pictures, they found *flint* and bone fragments used to carve the pictures and *pigments* used to create colors. Like *fossils*, the materials were sealed in the layers of the ground.

After a great deal of study the scientists finally understood what the boys had found. The pictures on the wall had been created by Stone Age people who lived about 17,000 years earlier.

---

创作时期（使用木炭创作的画可以通过测量木炭的变化程度来确定创作时间）。但他们发现这些画作无法用这种方法来确定创作时间。

科学家们只好观察洞穴低处来寻找答案。在画作下面的地上，他们找到了用来雕刻画作的火石和骨头碎片，以及着色用的颜料。这些材料像化石一样被密封在不同的地层里。

经过大量的研究，科学家们终于明白孩子们发现的是什么了。墙壁上的画是17,000年以前，由石器时代的人创作出来的。

---

radiocarbon *n.* 放射性碳  
pigment *n.* 颜料  
flint *n.* 火石  
fossil *n.* 化石

◆ WHAT THE BOYS FOUND

**WORLD MYSTERIES**

### Who Painted the Caves?

Still, like other caves in the area, the Lascaux cave held many more secrets.

Scientists wondered who these artists were. Why had they carved and painted pictures so far underground?

Scientists in 1940 already knew a great deal about Stone Age people. Stone Age men were *hunters* who killed and ate large animals like *bison*. They were also people who believed in the magical powers of their leader, the Shaman.

Scientists wondered if the pictures on the walls of the Lascaux cave could possibly have been carved and painted by a Shaman.

---

是谁在洞穴里画画？

如同本地其他的洞穴一样，拉斯科洞穴仍有很多未解之谜。

科学家们还不知道这些艺术家们是谁。为什么他们在这么长的地下通道雕刻和创作了这些画作？

1940年时，科学家们已经知道了许多关于石器时代的事情。石器时代的人捕杀并且食用大型的动物，比如野牛。他们相信他们的领袖——萨满祭司——有着神奇的力量。

科学家们想知道拉斯科洞穴墙壁上的画作是不是萨满祭司一人能够完成的。这位有着神秘力量的领袖是否能够走到地下与以前居住在此的人的

---

hunter *n.* 猎人　　　　　　　　　　　　　　　　bison *n.* 野牛

♦ WHAT THE BOYS FOUND

Could this mystical leader have gone underground to try to communicate with spirits of people who had lived before? Could he have painted the pictures to ensure a successful hunt?

Or could the hunters themselves have created the pictures as a way to bring them luck on their hunt? In other nearby caves, scientists found small and large footprints. Did this mean that children helped the artists or came to visit the Shaman with their parents?

One question really *befuddled* the scientists. How were the artists able to see? It was very dark deep inside the cave, and no one believed that Stone Age people used lighting that could be carried into the cave. So, did the Stone Age people come first and the people who did the paintings follow much later, after fire had been *discovered*?

---

灵魂进行交流？他是否能够画出这些画作来确保捕猎的成功？

或者猎人们自己能不能创作这些画来为捕猎祈求好运？在其他临近的洞穴里，科学家们发现了大大小小的脚印。这是否意味着小孩子们帮助过艺术家，或者和他们的父母一起来拜访过萨满祭司？

有一个问题确实使科学家们感到迷惑。艺术家们是如何看到东西的？洞穴内部极其昏暗，目前无法证明石器时代的人可以将光源搬进洞穴。所以，是不是石器时代的人先在这里生活，然后在很久以后人类发明了火，画作的作者们才来到洞穴的？

---

befuddle *v.* 使迷惑　　　　　　　　　　discover *v.* 发现

**WORLD MYSTERIES**

As with many questions that seem to have no answers, this one was solved by accident. Someone found a piece of sandstone that was *hollowed* out on one side. Inside the hollowed out circle was some left-over carbon. When the carbon was analyzed and dated, scientists found traces of animal fat.

The lighting mystery was solved. Stone Age artists lit their workspace by burning lamps filled with animal fat.

But other questions remained. How did the artists manage to carve and paint the *glorious* pictures at the top of the Painted Gallery? The ceiling in the gallery is very, very high and really impossible to reach. Could those holes halfway up the wall hold the answer?

---

许多看起来无解的问题都是在无意间得到答案的，这个问题也是一样。有人发现了一片砂岩，有一侧被挖空了。在挖空的部分有剩余的木炭。当这些木炭被分析和追溯之后，科学家们发现了动物脂肪的痕迹。

照明之谜得以解开。石器时代的艺术家们就是点燃盛满动物脂肪的灯来给洞穴照明的。

但仍然有其他的问题未解。这些艺术家们是怎样做到在油画馆穴顶进行壮美的雕刻和作画的？洞穴顶部非常非常高，几乎不可能触及。在墙的上半部的那些小孔里，我们能找到答案吗？

---

hollow *v.* 挖空　　　　　　　　　　　　　glorious *adj.* 壮丽的

◆ WHAT THE BOYS FOUND

Scientists estimated the size of the artists. They guessed how far the artists were from those high paintings. When they were finished guessing, they *deduced* the answer. The holes were used for a temporary *scaffold* that the artists climbed or stood on as they painted.

What were Stone Age artists like? How did they create color? What tools did they use? What were they thinking?

Luckily the artists left all kinds of *clues* behind on the ground below their masterpieces.

Can you guess what tools they used to carve the stone walls inside the cave?

The answer is ... they used more than one kind of tool, depending

---

科学家们估算了艺术家的身高。他们对艺术家同高处的那些画作之间的距离做了猜测。在猜测之后，他们推导出了答案。墙上的小孔用来搭建临时的脚手架，艺术家们爬上去或站上去来画画。

石器时代的艺术家们什么样子？他们如何制作颜色？用什么工具？他们的思想是怎样的？

幸运的是，这些艺术家们在他们杰作下方的地面上留下了各种各样的线索。

你能猜出他们用什么工具在洞穴的石壁上进行雕刻吗？

答案是……他们的工具不止一种，用多少工具取决于他们所刻的石壁

---

deduce *v.* 推断　　　　　　　　　　　scaffold *n.* 脚手架
clue *n.* 线索

## WORLD MYSTERIES

on the kind of rock they were carving. If the rock was very soft, they used a stick or their finger. If the rock was very hard, they carved a pointed or rounded stone tool to cut into the rock face.

Other rock faces were impossible to carve at all and had to be painted. Most of the pictures are painted with red and black *pigments* made from *minerals* and metals found in the earth.

### Understanding the Cave Art

What else do the caves tell us? Do we know what the carvings and paintings mean?

---

材质。如果石壁很软,他们就用木棍或者手指。如果石壁很硬,他们就使用带尖角的或者圆形的石器来切割石壁表面。

有些石壁实在无法雕刻,就只能用颜料作画。大部分的作品涂的颜料为红色与黑色,这些颜料来自于在泥土中发现的矿物及金属。

理解洞穴艺术

洞穴还能给我们什么信息?我们是否知道这些雕刻和画作的含义?

---

pigment *n.* 颜料　　　　　　　　　　　　　　mineral *n.* 矿物

◆ WHAT THE BOYS FOUND

One thing that the caves tell us is that men, women, and children have always drawn pictures and always will. Stone Age people did not live in these caves. They went down into the earth and created pictures that *represented* something in their lives. Whether they went there just to draw or to be near their *ancestors* who lived before or to seek help from their Shaman, we may never know. But they were still creating art.

---

洞穴告诉我们的一条信息是：男人、女人和孩子时刻都在作画。石器时代的人不住在这些洞穴里。他们来到地下，创作了这些画作来反映他们生活的点滴。无论他们到那里只是为了作画，或者为了接近他们曾经在此居住的祖先，还是要从萨满祭司那里寻求帮助，我们也许永远都不会知道真相。但无论原因何在，他们都创造了艺术。

---

represent *v.* 代表　　　　　　　　　　　　　ancestor *n.* 祖先

WORLD MYSTERIES

# 4

# Mysteries of the Lost Civilization

**The Island of Crete**

South of Greece there is a large island called Crete. The island has many mountains. It is in a beautiful part of the Mediterranean Sea called the Aegean Sea. Today, Crete is a part of the country of Greece, but long ago Crete was its own nation. It was home to a great group of people and culture known as the Minoan *civilization*.

Between the years of about 2600 B.C. and 1450 B.C., the

---

# 消失的文明之谜

**克里特岛**

希腊的南边有一个很大的岛，叫作克里特岛。岛上有很多山。它属于地中海上美丽的爱琴海的一部分。如今，克里特岛是希腊的一部分。但是，很久以前，它是一个独立的国家。它是一群被称作克里特人的家园，是克里特文化的发祥地。

公元前2600年到1450年之间，米诺斯文明在克里特岛上繁荣起来。

---

**civilization** *n.* 文明

◆ MYSTERIES OF THE LOST CIVILIZATION

Minoan civilization *prospered* on Crete. Hundreds of years of trading with other countries around the Mediterranean Sea had made the Minoans rich. Then it seemed as though the Minoan civilization disappeared overnight. A mystery was born. How could a rich nation that was a leader among other nations, suddenly disappear?

Someone You Should Know

In Greek *mythology*, Minos was the son of the Greek god Zeus and ruled the island of Crete from his palace at Knossos. The word "Minoan" means "of Minos." One of the first people to study the ancient civilization on Crete named it "Minoan" after King Minos. Some research suggests there might be some truth in stories from Greek mythology. Some researchers think Minos was a title given to all rulers of Crete during the time period from about 3000 B.C. to 1000 B.C. known as the Bronze Age.

---

几百年来，与地中海沿岸其他国家的贸易往来使米诺斯人富裕起来。之后，似乎一夜之间，米诺斯文明消失了。谜团诞生了，一个众国之中如此富裕的发达国家怎么会突然消失了呢？

你需要了解的人

在希腊神话中，米诺斯是希腊宙斯神的儿子，住在克诺索斯王宫并统治着克里特岛。"Minoan"意为"米诺斯的"。第一批研究克里特古文明的一个研究者，就以米诺斯国王的名字命名"克里特岛人"。一些研究者认为希腊神话故事可能有些是事实。还有一些研究人员认为，米诺斯是公元前3000年到1000年之间，也就是青铜时期，授予克里特岛上统治者们的头衔。

---

prosper v. 繁荣                                    mythology n. 神话

**WORLD MYSTERIES**

◆ MYSTERIES OF THE LOST CIVILIZATION

## The First People in Crete

The first people on Crete probably *settled* on the island about 8,000 years ago. Researchers believe they came from the area known today as Turkey. Since Crete is an island, people had to use ships to settle there. These people would have brought their knowledge of farming and of the sea.

Researchers have learned that the soil on Crete was good for growing food. The Minoans raised sheep and grew *olives* and grapes. As the people's ability to create goods (such as olive oil, wine, and wool) grew, so did their civilization. The island's forests were full of trees that were cut down for wood. The Minoans used the wood to build ships. They used the ships to carry goods to trade with other nations.

---

克里特岛上的土著人

早在8000年前，克里特岛上的土著人就定居于此了。研究者们认为他们来自如今的土耳其。既然克里特是座岛，人们不得不使用船只。这些人也带来了耕地和海洋知识。

研究人员已证明，克里特岛上的土壤特别适合种植业。米诺斯人饲养羊，种植橄榄和葡萄。随着人们制造技术的提高（如生产橄榄油、红酒和羊毛），文明程度也随之提升了。岛上森林浓密，可以砍伐树木获得木材。米诺斯人用木头造船。他们用船运输货物与其他国家进行贸易。

---

settle *v.* 定居      olive *n.* 橄榄

**WORLD MYSTERIES**

### The Minoan Culture

By about 3000 B.C., the Minoans had become great traders. The Minoans traded their goods with their Mediterranean neighbors for *gemstones*, *ivory*, silver, gold, and copper. These things were not found on Crete so the people valued them. The Minoans grew rich through trade.

The Minoan civilization became more advanced over time. They had a system of writing and created many fine works of art, such as *frescoes*, *pottery*, and jewelry. They built more towns and connected the towns with paved roads. They built storehouses to keep the goods to be traded. They built fine houses and large palaces. The

---

米诺斯文化

到公元前3000年，米诺斯人已经成为名副其实的商人。米诺斯人和地中海附近的人频繁交易，交换的物品包括雕刻的宝石、象牙、金、银和铜。因为这些东西在岛上没有被发现，所以克里特岛人很珍视它们。米诺斯人通过贸易变得富裕起来。

随着时间的推移，米诺斯文明变得更加先进。他们有了一套文字书写体系，创造出很多精美的艺术品，如壁画、陶器和珠宝。他们建造了更多的城镇，各城之间用石铺的街道连接。他们盖了仓库来储存货物以备交

---

gemstone *n.* （经切割打磨的）宝石　　　　ivory *n.* 象牙
fresco *n.* 壁画　　　　　　　　　　　　　　pottery *n.* 陶器

### MYSTERIES OF THE LOST CIVILIZATION

palaces became the centers of society.

Much of what we know about the Minoan civilization is a *theory*. A theory is an idea or a group of ideas based on evidence. Examples of *evidence* are objects such as buildings or art that can be studied by researchers.

Researchers looked at the type of gems used in Minoan jewelry and then found the mountains from which the gems were mined. Researchers also studied the type of *clay* used in the pottery. Frescoes and pottery are important pieces of evidence that often show how people lived. Many Minoan works of art show scenes of daily life.

Minoan frescoes and pottery show the people farming, sailing, and celebrating. They show how Minoans dressed and wore their

---

易。他们建造了漂亮的房子和宏伟的王宫。王宫成为社会中心。

关于米诺斯文明，我们进一步了解到的是一种理论。理论是基于证据之上的一个或一些观点。证据的例子就是能够被研究者用来当作研究的事物，如建筑或艺术。

研究者通过米诺斯人珠宝上的宝石类型，发现了蕴藏这些宝石的山脉。研究者还研究了他们的陶器中的黏土类型。壁画和陶器通常是展现人们生活方式的最重要的证据。许多米诺斯艺术品再现了他们的日常生活片段。

米诺斯壁画和陶器再现了米诺斯人耕作、航行和庆祝的场面。他们展

---

theory *n.* 理论　　　　　　　　　　　　evidence *n.* 证据
clay *n.* 黏土

## WORLD MYSTERIES

hair. Another important piece to understanding the Minoans is that their frescoes and pottery show few scenes of battles. This tells researchers that the Minoan people were mostly peaceful and had few enemies who *challenged* their power.

The Minoan civilization reached its *peak* in the years after about 1700 B.C. Then, beginning in about 1450 B.C., the civilization *collapsed*. There is evidence that many of its cities and palaces burned. By about 1100 B.C., the Minoan civilization no longer existed.

Researchers have tried to solve the mystery of what happened to the Minoans by studying the evidence. For a long time, many historians thought a *volcano* was the cause.

---

现了米诺斯人的服饰和发型。另一个重要的证据是，壁画和陶器几乎没有表现战争的场面。这向研究者证明，米诺斯人都很爱好和平，很少与人为敌。

公元前1700年后的几年里，米诺斯文明达到了巅峰。然后，大约开始于公元前1450年，米诺斯文明瓦解了。有证据表明，许多城市和宫殿被烧。到公元前1100年，米诺斯文明不再存在。

研究人员已经努力地去揭开米诺斯文明消失的谜团。很长时间以来，许多历史学家认为火山是这背后的原因。

---

challenge *v.* 向……挑战  
collapse *v.* 瓦解

peak *n.* 顶峰  
volcano *n.* 火山

◆ MYSTERIES OF THE LOST CIVILIZATION

WORLD MYSTERIES

### The Explosion of Thera

The Minoans lived near an island called Thera (now called Santorini). The island was about 70 miles (40 km) north of Crete. The island of Thera had been an active volcano off and on for many thousands of years. But then the volcano became quiet long enough for people to think the island was safe, so people built cities there. However, a large amount of *magma* was building deep beneath the island. (Magma is melted rock mixed with hot gases.) The build-up of magma caused great pressure within the mountain island. The pressure caused the land to shake, causing earthquakes. Then one day, after several earthquakes, Thera blew its top!

The *eruption* of Thera was one of the most powerful eruptions in history. You may have seen pictures of Mount Saint Helens, the

---

锡拉火山爆发

米诺斯人住在锡拉岛（现在叫作圣托里尼）附近，它距克里特岛北部大约有70英里（40公里）。几千年来，锡拉岛一直是一座周期性喷发的活火山。但是，这座火山沉寂了好久，以致人们认为这座岛是安全的，所以在那里建造城市。然而，大量的岩浆正在岛的深处形成。（岩浆是熔化的岩石和热气混合而成的物质。）岩浆的逐渐累积导致了火山内部的压力。压力致使大地摇动，进而引发地震。于是在几次地震过后的某一天，锡拉火山喷发了！

锡拉火山的喷发是历史上最强有力的火山喷发之一。你可能已经看过1980年，圣海伦火山在华盛顿州喷发时的图片。那是一次不小的火山喷

---

magma *n.* 岩浆　　　　　　　　　　　　eruption *n.* 喷发；爆发

◆ MYSTERIES OF THE LOST CIVILIZATION

volcano that erupted in Washington State in 1980. That was a big eruption, but it was tiny compared to Thera.

The eruption of Thera was about twelve times bigger than the eruption of Mount Saint Helens. Large amounts of rock, hot gases, and ashes were blown from inside the volcano into the skies above it. Rocks and ash fell onto the islands throughout the Aegean Sea. Small rocks, gases, and ash formed a *gigantic* dark cloud.

Thera's eruption was so large it caused a large sea wave called a tsunami. The wave may have been 100 feet high, or even higher. The tsunami *crashed* into shores around the Mediterranean. The land on many islands was covered with water. Farms and even whole cities were lost.

After the eruption, all that was left of the middle of the island of Thera was a large hole. A large hole caused by the collapse of a

---

发，但是与锡拉火山喷发相比，真是小巫见大巫。

锡拉火山的喷发程度比圣海伦火山的喷发程度大上12倍还要多。大量的岩石、热气和灰烬从火山内部喷涌而出，笼罩着上空。岩石和灰烬涌入了爱琴海流域的许多岛屿。小的岩石、热气和灰烬形成了巨大的黑云。

锡拉火山的喷发如此猛烈，形成了大的海浪，即海啸。海浪可能高达100英尺，甚至更高。海啸猛烈地袭击了地中海流域的海岸。许多岛屿的陆地被洪水淹没。耕地，甚至整个城市消失了。

火山爆发后，只留下了锡拉岛中间的一个大洞。由火山喷发导致的大

---

gigantic  *adj.*  巨大的                                           crash  *v.*  猛撞

# WORLD MYSTERIES

volcano is called a *caldera*. The caldera filled up with water from the sea. The island of Thera became the shape of a *crescent*.

### The Greek *Invasion*

Beginning in about 1450 B.C., Crete was invaded by people from Greece. They were called the Mycenaeans. It was probably the Mycenaeans who struck the final blow that ended the Minoan civilization. The Minoans were weakened by the eruption of Thera. They could not gather the strength they needed to keep themselves safe from the Mycenaeans.

The Mycenaeans were fighters. They took over cities. Researchers know this because tales of their fights were written down. These writings can be read today.

---

洞叫做火山口。火山口充满了海水。锡拉岛变成了新月形。

希腊入侵

大约在公元前1450年,克里特岛遭到了来自希腊人的入侵。他们被叫作迈锡尼人,他们的入侵给了米诺斯文明消亡最后一击。锡拉火山喷发削弱了米诺斯文明。他们无法聚集力量来抵御迈锡尼人的入侵。

迈锡尼人是勇猛的战士,他们占领了城镇。研究人员通过一些文字材料了解到这一点。今天,这些关于战斗的文字材料都可以看到。

---

caldera *n.* 火山口      crescent *n.* 新月
invasion *n.* 入侵

◆ MYSTERIES OF THE LOST CIVILIZATION

**Did Thera Destroy the Minoans?**

For a long time, researchers thought that the eruption of Thera caused the *disappearance* of the Minoans on Crete. They believed the two events happened at the same time. However, later evidence showed that the volcano on Thera erupted about 180 years before the Minoans disappeared. So did that make researchers think the volcano theory was wrong? Well, not exactly.

Some researchers now think that the eruption of Thera may have played a part in the Minoans' disappearance. Thera's eruption may have weakened the Minoans. The tsunami would have destroyed many of the Minoan ships and ports along Crete's shores and ruined crops as well. This would have left the Minoans with few goods to trade and few trading ships. The earthquakes before the eruption could have destroyed Crete's cities as well. All these losses would have made the people who *survived* very sad. They would have had

---

是锡拉火山摧毁了米诺斯人吗？

很久以来，研究人员认为是锡拉火山爆发导致了克里特岛上米诺斯人的消失。他们认为两件事是同时发生的。然而，最近的证据表明，锡拉火山的爆发发生在米诺斯人消失的大约180年前。那么，事实让研究人员否定了火山喷发学说的可靠性吗？当然，并不完全如此。

如今，一些研究人员认为，锡拉火山的喷发可能对米诺斯人的消失起了一定作用。锡拉火山喷发也许削弱了米诺斯文明。海啸损坏了许多米诺斯船只和克里特海岸港口，同时被摧毁的还有庄稼。留给米诺斯人用来交易的，只有为数不多的货物和贸易船只。海啸前的地震也摧毁了克里特岛上的城市。所有这一切使活下来的人感到非常的沮丧。他们不得不去找

---

disappearance  *n.*  消失                                survive  *v.*  存活；幸存

## WORLD MYSTERIES

to find lots of money and energy to *rebuild* Crete. These losses made Crete open to enemies like it had never been before.

**Was Crete Atlantis?**

Many people are beginning to think that Homer's tales are real stories. They think the tales tell about real cities and real people who lived a very long time ago. They think that if Homer's stories have some truth, then perhaps other ancient writers' tales are also true.

An old Greek philosopher (deep thinker) named Plato told a very interesting story. He said there was once a great island country that disappeared. He called the country Atlantis. Plato said Atlantis had been destroyed by a terrible *disaster*. The disaster caused the country to sink under the sea, never to be seen again.

---

到更多的钱和能源来重建克里特。这些损失使得克里特首次向敌人开放自己。

克里特是亚特兰蒂斯吗？

许多人因此认为，荷马描述的故事确有其事。他们认为故事讲述的城市和人们，的确在很久以前存在过。他们认为如果荷马的故事包含一些真相，那么也许其他古代作家的作品也是真的。

一位叫作柏拉图的古希腊哲学家（深刻的思想家）讲述了这样一个有趣的故事。他讲道，曾经有一个很大的消失的岛国。他称它亚特兰蒂斯。亚特兰蒂斯在一场可怕的灾难中被摧毁。灾难导致整个国家沉入海底，从此再也没有出现过。

---

rebuild *v.* 重建　　　　　　　　　　　　　　　　disaster *n.* 灾难

◆ MYSTERIES OF THE LOST CIVILIZATION

According to Plato, Atlantis was larger than Libya and Asia combined (larger than the continental United States). He wrote that Atlantis's kings, who were descended from the sea and earthquake god Poseidon, had power over the *entire* known world.

Plato's Atlantis

Plato wrote about Atlantis twice about a *decade* or so before his death in 348 B.C. He wrote of an *ideal* civilization that existed millions of years before the time of his writing.

Because of the greatness of Minoan Crete and the fact that it seemed to disappear, some people think it may be Plato's Atlantis. Some people think that by studying Plato's stories about Atlantis,

---

依据柏拉图，亚特兰蒂斯比利比亚和亚洲加起来还要大（比美国大陆大得多）。他写道，亚特兰蒂斯的国王们是海神兼地震神波塞东的后代，拥有掌管整个世界的权力。

柏拉图的亚特兰蒂斯

柏拉图在公元前348年死去之前的十年间，两次提及过亚特兰蒂斯。他提到，在他写作之前，一个非常理想的文明曾存在了上百万年。

正是由于米诺斯克里特文明的伟大，和它看似消失的事实，一些人认为它可能就是柏拉图笔下的亚特兰蒂斯。一些人认为，通过研究柏拉图关

---

entire *adj.* 整个的
ideal *adj.* 理想的

decade *n.* 十年

**WORLD MYSTERIES**

they can learn more about the collapse of the Minoan civilization.

Whether or not Crete was Atlantis, many people are *intrigued* by both mysteries. They like finding a way to solve them. Researchers study evidence in hopes that they might put a piece of the puzzle of Atlantis and the disappearance of Minoan Crete in place. Maybe there will not be an answer to what really happened, but one thing is sure—the search for answers will continue.

于亚特兰蒂斯的故事，他们能够知道关于米诺斯文明瓦解的更多资料。

克里特是否是亚特兰蒂斯？许多人被这两个不解之谜所吸引。他们希望找到获得答案的方法。研究者研究迹象，希望能将亚特兰蒂斯之谜和米诺斯克里特消失之谜对号入座。也许答案永远都难以获得，但有一事是确定无疑的——对答案的探索不会停止。

intrigue  v.  激起……的好奇心

◆ MUMMIES

# Mummies

### Introduction

In modern countries around the world, including Egypt, people are often buried in *coffins* after they die. Sometimes the body is *cremated*, and the ashes are either kept by loved ones or spread over an area that the person enjoyed, such as the ocean. But this is not the way it has always been. The ancient Egyptians turned their dead into *mummies*.

The ancient Egyptians are famous for making mummies. They mummified everyone from kings to pets by drying the bodies,

---

## 木乃伊

### 介绍

世界上包括埃及在内的现代国家，人们死去后都是放入棺材中埋葬的。有时尸体被火化，骨灰可以交给亲人们保存或洒向死者热爱的地方，比如说大海。但古人处理尸体的方法有所不同。古埃及人会把尸体做成木乃伊。

古埃及人因制作木乃伊而闻名于世。他们把每具尸体都制作成木乃伊，从国王到宠物无一例外。他们烘干尸体，用香料摩擦尸体，然后用布

---

coffin *n.* 棺材　　　　　　　　　　　　cremate *v.* 火化
mummy *n.* 木乃伊

WORLD MYSTERIES

◆ MUMMIES

rubbing them with spices, and *wrapping* them in strips of cloth. However, the Egyptians are not the only people that mummified their dead. There is evidence of mummification in many places around the world.

What Are Mummies?

A mummy is a *preserved* corpse. Normally, a dead body decays very quickly. *Bacteria* in the air start decomposing body cells immediately after death. If the body is left alone, scavengers and pests, like vultures and flies, devour the corpse. In a mummy, the decay process is arrested, and the dead body is preserved for thousands of years.

The first mummification occurred naturally, in areas that were too dry or cold for bacteria to grow. The body was preserved without

条布卷起来。然而，埃及人并不是唯一将尸体制成木乃伊的人。在世界各地都有制作木乃伊的迹象。

什么是木乃伊？

木乃伊就是保存下来的尸体。通常来说，尸体腐烂非常迅速。生物死亡后，空气中的细菌立即开始分解尸体的细胞。如果置之不管，像秃鹰和苍蝇这样的食腐动物和害虫就会吞食尸体。而在木乃伊身上就不会发生这样的事情，尸体可以保存数千年。

最初，干尸是在太过干燥或者太过寒冷的地区自然形成的，细菌在这些地方无法存活。不用人工参与，尸体就可以完好保存。随后，人们开始

wrap *v.* 包；裹  
bacteria *n.* 细菌

preserve *v.* 保存

# WORLD MYSTERIES

human *interference*. Later on, people developed ways to preserve mummies *artificially*.

### Mummification

The first Egyptian mummies were buried in the hot desert sand. It was so dry that the bodies dried out almost immediately, preserving them from decay. These dried mummies looked a lot like beef jerky. Their flesh became tough and hard.

Unfortunately, unprotected bodies buried in the desert were often eaten by *jackals*, which love the taste of "human jerky." Egyptians tried to protect their buried ancestors by covering the burial site with rocks. Wealthier Egyptians buried family members in painted coffins. But the coffins, which kept out the jackals, also kept out the hot sand, and the bodies inside decayed.

---

人工制作木乃伊。

木乃伊的制作过程

最早的埃及木乃伊埋葬在炎热的沙漠里。由于太过干燥，尸体几乎一下子就失去了全部水分，使它不至于腐烂。这些风干的木乃伊看上去非常像牛肉干。他们的肉变得又糙又硬。

不幸的是，未被保护而埋葬在炎热沙漠里的尸体大部分被豺狼吃掉了，这些豺狼喜欢"人肉干"的味道。埃及人试图用石头盖在他们祖先的尸体上用以保护尸体。富有一点的埃及人用漆过的棺材给他们的家庭成员下葬，在阻止豺狼的同时也阻止了火热的沙子，棺材内的尸体就腐烂了。

---

interference *n.* 干涉　　　　　　　　　　artificially *adv.* 人工地
jackal *n.* 豺

◆ MUMMIES

*Resourceful* Egyptians developed ways to preserve the bodies before burial. When someone died, the body was given to a team of *embalmers*. First, the embalmers laid the body face up on a six-foot-wide embalming table. Their first job was to remove all the soft *organs* that encouraged the growth of bacteria. They carefully pulled the brain out through the nose with an embalming hook, making sure not to deform the person's face. The brain was not very important to the ancient Egyptians. They believed that the heart was the most and feeling.

The chief embalmer cut an incision in the left side of the stomach. From this hole, the embalming team pulled out all the internal organs except the heart and placed them to the side. The stomach, liver, lungs, and intestines were preserved individually in special jars called

---

足智多谋的埃及人在埋葬尸体前想尽办法保存尸体。当有人死去时，就把尸体交给一组尸体防腐者处理。首先，尸体防腐者将尸体正面朝上放在六英尺宽的防腐桌子上。他们的第一个任务就是移除所有易被细菌感染的柔软器官。他们用涂钩把死者的大脑小心地从鼻子处勾出来，并确保不损坏死者的面部。对于古埃及人来说大脑并不十分重要。他们坚信心脏是最重要的器官，认为那里才是思想和感觉的中枢。

尸体防腐者首领将尸体胃的左部切开。从这个洞里，全组人掏出除心脏以外的所有器官，置于一旁。胃部、肺部、肾脏和肠子将单独保存在一

---

resourceful *adj.* 足智多谋的　　　embalmer *n.* （尸体）防腐处理者
organ *n.* 器官

**WORLD MYSTERIES**

canopic jars. These organs accompanied the body during burial but were not as important as the heart. The heart was preserved inside the body.

Embalmers washed the body, inside and out, with palm wine. The alcohol in wine killed bacteria. By this time, the body had probably begun to *stink*, a sign of decay. So the embalmers filled the body with bags of sweet-smelling spices mixed with natron, a special salt. Then they covered up the body and internal organs with more natron and left them alone for 40 days.

The whole mummification process took 70 days. Once the drying process had been completed, the embalmers removed the salt. The mummy became very light, since all the water—which made up over 65 percent of the body's weight—had been removed. The

个特殊的卡诺皮克罐中。这些器官在葬礼上都和尸体放在一起，但它们都没有心脏重要，心脏保存在尸体内部。

尸体防腐者们用棕榈酒清洗尸体的内部和外部。酒精能够杀死细菌。此时，尸体有可能开始发出臭味，这是腐败的征兆。所以尸体防腐者们将尸体塞满香料和天然碳酸钠的混合物质（一种特别的盐）。然后他们用更多的盐覆在尸体和器官上，放置40天。

整个干尸制作过程用时70天。当烘干尸体这一步完成时，尸体防腐者们将盐移除。木乃伊变得特别轻，因为身体的水分都被移除了，而水分

stink  *v.*  发出恶臭味

◆ MUMMIES

embalmers filled the inside of a corpse with linen stuffing, producing a body that appeared strong and healthy instead of *shriveled*. Then they rubbed the corpse with more spices, mixed with wax and oil, to make it smell sweet. Next, a sticky resin made of tree sap was poured over the body. When the resin hardened, it formed a thin, protective shell around the body. This shell protected the mummy from bacteria and caused it to become darker in color.

Embalmers often applied makeup to the mummy's face to make it look more *alive*. They also placed jewelry on a rich person's corpse before wrapping it up. The resin-soaked wrap consisted of linen *bandages* the length of a football field. The wrap helped to preserve the shape of the body.

---

占体重的65%。尸体防腐者们将尸体内部填充满亚麻布填塞物，让尸体看上去强壮健康而不是干瘪不堪。然后他们用更多的香料来摩擦尸体，混合着蜡和油，让它闻起来很香。接下来，用树的汁液做的粘树脂淋在尸体上。当树脂硬了的时候，它就变成了一层包裹在尸体外面的厚厚的保护壳。这种保护壳使细菌不再侵袭尸体，也使颜色变得更加暗沉。

尸体防腐者们也经常在木乃伊的脸上涂抹一些化妆品使它看起来有生气。他们也经常在裹起尸体之前，在富人的脖子上戴上珠宝。树脂浸渍的裹尸绷带面积可足足覆盖、整个足球场。用它来包裹尸体是为了防止尸体变形。

---

shrivel *v.* 皱缩　　　　　　　　　　　alive *adj.* 有生气的
bandage *n.* 绷带

## WORLD MYSTERIES

The best linen was saved for the outermost layer of bandages. Cheap linen was used on the inside, where it couldn't be seen. Magical charms and talismans meant to ensure the mummy's safety in the *realm* of the dead were put between the layers of bandages. These talismans were carved out of precious stones. Talismans are small objects instilled with magical protections.

The *STEPS* OF MUMMIFICATION

1. Place the body on a large table, facing up.
2. Remove internal organs through a cut in the *abdomen*.
3. Wash the body with palm wine.
4. Dry the body by covering it with piles of salt.

---

最好的亚麻布用来包裹在绷带的最外层。廉价的亚麻布包在里面看不见的地方。有魔法的符咒和护身符意在确保木乃伊在来世的安全，放在绷带层之间。这些护身符是由珠宝雕刻的。护身符是有着护身魔力的小物品。

制作木乃伊的步骤
1. 将尸体正面朝上放在大桌子上。
2. 切开腹部取出内脏。
3. 用棕榈酒清洗尸体。
4. 用大量的盐干燥尸体。

---

realm *n.* 领域；范围
abdomen *n.* 腹部

step *n.* 步骤

5. Remove the salt, and rub the body with sweet *herbs*.

6. Stuff the body with linen and bags of spices.

7. Cover the body with resin.

8. Apply makeup and jewelry.

9. Wrap the body in bandages.

### The Afterlife

The ancient Egyptians believed that immortality depended on having a well-preserved body. They believed that a dead person split up at the moment of death into several parts: the ba, the ka, and the physical body. The ka was a person's ghostly identical twin. It lived inside the mummified heart and could not move from the tomb. The

---

5. 去除盐，并用有香草填满尸体内部。

6. 用亚麻布和香料包填充尸体。

7. 用树脂涂满尸体。

8. 给尸体化妆，戴上珠宝。

9. 用绷带包裹好尸体。

来生

古埃及人认为，不朽建立在完好保存尸体的基础之上。他们相信人在死亡瞬间分离成几部分：灵魂，灵体，和肉身。灵体是一个人魂魄的双胞胎，它住在干尸的心脏里，谁也不能将它移去。灵魂代表了人的品格和精

---

herb  *n.*  草本植物

## WORLD MYSTERIES

ba, which represented the personality and spirit of a person, was a human-headed bird that could fly around freely by day. The ba and the ka joined to form the akh, a person's soul.

According to ancient Egyptian belief, a dead person's soul traveled through the dangerous realm of the dead to a special palace of judgment, called Osiris's palace. Along the way, the soul *dodged* monstrous snakes and crocodiles while crossing huge rivers of fire. Osiris, the god of the dead, judged everyone by weighing their hearts on a scale. If a person's heart was heavy with sin, it was thrown to the hungry monster beneath the scales. That person would die permanently. But if the heart was lighter than a feather, then the dead person would live forever—or be immortal—in the world of Osiris.

---

神，它是一个人首鸟身的形象，在死去的那一整天自由地在空中盘旋。灵体和灵魂构成了akh，一个人的灵魂。

　　根据古埃及人的信仰，人死后，灵魂要穿过一个危险的死亡国度到达一个特殊的审判宫殿，叫作"奥西里斯宫殿"。在路上，穿越火河的时候，灵魂要躲避巨大的蛇和鳄鱼。奥西里斯是死亡之神，用天平称量每个人心脏的重量来判断人的好坏。如果一个人的心因罪恶而沉重，这颗心脏就直接被扔到了天平下面喂饥饿的怪物，这个人就永远地离去了。但如果一个人的心比羽毛还轻的话，这个人就会获得永生——或者不朽——这就是奥西里斯统治的世界。

---

dodge  *v.*  躲开

◆ MUMMIES

When the Egyptians first began to make mummies, only very rich or important people were mummified. They believed that only *pharaohs* and nobles deserved an afterlife.

However, as the embalming process became easier and the Egyptians became richer, more people were mummified. The Egyptians eventually believed that everyone deserved to have a chance at immortality.

Since the Egyptians believed that the afterlife was exactly like life, they buried mummies with their favorite objects and tools. Wealthy nobles were buried with gold and *gems*. Children were buried with their favorite toys. Everyone was buried with *clay* representations of food and drink, and with clay figurines called shabtis—servants who would work for them in the afterlife.

---

当埃及人最早开始制作木乃伊的时候，只有富有的人和重要的人才有资格被制成木乃伊。他们认为只有法老和贵族们才有资格拥有来生。

然而，尸体防腐的工艺越来越纯熟，埃及人也变得越来越富有，越来越多的人死后被制成了木乃伊。埃及人最终相信每个人都有不朽的机会。

因为埃及人相信人死后的生活就像现实生活一样，他们将死者最喜爱的工具和物品同木乃伊一起埋葬。富有的贵族们用金子和宝石陪葬，儿童们同他们最喜欢的玩具一起埋葬。每个人的墓穴里都有由泥土代表的食物和饮品，也有泥土制成的小雕像叫作"沙伯替"——在来生会服侍他们的仆人。

---

pharaoh *n.* 法老　　　　　　　　　　　　　　　　gem *n.* 宝石
clay *n.* 黏土

**WORLD MYSTERIES**

**The Burial**

Mummies were laid to rest in decorated coffins usually made of papier-maché and beaten gold. Richer people were buried in a *sarcophagus* made of stone or a coffin of imported wood. Pharaohs were buried in up to four gold-covered coffins nested inside each other.

The coffins were painted with a representation of the person's face so that the ba could find the right tomb when it returned at night.

Hieroglyphs, painted or *chiseled* onto the coffin, told the story of the person's life. These inscriptions also held spells to keep the dead person safe in the underworld.

*Superstitions* were common in Egypt. Most people believed

---

葬礼

木乃伊被放置在一个装饰华丽、由纸浆和金箔做成的棺材里面安息。富有的人则葬在石棺里，或是用上好木材打造的棺材里。法老则被葬在由四个金面棺材嵌在一起的棺材里。

棺材上画着代表死者面部的画像，这样灵魂在夜晚归来的时候就会找到正确的坟墓了。

象形文字被画在或者刻在棺材上，讲述死者的生平。这些碑文上也有咒语，用于保护死者在阴间的安全。

迷信在埃及很平常。绝大部分人相信木乃伊可以诅咒任何闯进墓穴和盗窃殉葬品的人。但盗贼们受到殉葬珍宝的诱惑，即使是防守最严密的墓

---

sarcophagus *n.* 石棺　　　　　　　　　　　　chisel *v.* 雕；刻
superstition *n.* 迷信

◆ MUMMIES

that mummies would *curse* anyone who disturbed their tomb and stole from the dead. But tempted by the treasures buried with the mummies, thieves broke into even the best-guarded tombs. They often *tore* the mummies apart, looking for the gold and gems under the bandages. They were willing to risk death and punishment for riches. Most tombs were robbed within a few years of their burials.

### The Tomb of Tutankhamen

The Pharaoh Tutankhamen, also called the Boy King, died when he was only 18. We know very little about his life or his rule in Egypt, but he is the most famous mummy in the world.

---

穴也不放过。他们经常将木乃伊撕扯开，寻找绷带下面的金子和宝石。他们愿意冒着被诅咒和死亡的危险来寻找财富。大部分的墓穴都在埋葬几年后就被洗劫一空了。

图坦卡蒙的坟墓

图坦卡蒙法老也被叫作"孩童国王"，他十八岁的时候就去世了。我们对他本人和他在埃及的统治几乎一无所知，但他却是世界上最有名的法老。

图坦卡蒙的墓穴在1923年被开启。即使在古时候被盗过两次，他的

---

curse *v.* 诅咒      tear *v.* 撕

## WORLD MYSTERIES

Tutankhamen's tomb was opened in 1923. Even though it had been robbed twice in ancient times, King Tut's tomb still held great treasures. The thieves had entered the second room, which was filled with Tut's gold *chariots* and statues. They stole about a sixth of the tomb's gold but were probably interrupted before they could finish. King Tut's mummy had not been touched.

King Tut was buried in a series of three coffins, one inside the other. The first two coffins were made of wood covered in bands of gold. But the innermost coffin was made of *solid* gold and covered with gems. Tut's beautiful burial mask was also made of pure gold. Heavy jeweled bracelets encircled his wrists, and golden amulets

---

墓穴仍然有大量宝藏。盗墓者进入了第二个房间，房间里装满了这位法老的金战车和雕像。他们几乎盗走了六分之一的宝藏，但可能在没有偷完时就遭遇了外来的干扰。图坦卡蒙的木乃伊没有被动过。

图坦王被埋葬在一个三层的棺材中，一个套着另一个。前两个棺材由木头制成表面全部是金子。但最里面的棺材是用纯金制成的，并有宝石覆盖在上面。图坦卡蒙的精美葬礼面具也是用纯金制成的。沉重的珠宝手镯环绕在他的手腕上，金质的护身符和项链成褶皱型环绕在他的脖子上。

---

chariot  n.  两轮无篷马车　　　　　　　　　　　　solid  adj.  纯质的

◆ MUMMIES

and necklaces were draped around his neck.

### Animal Mummies

The ancient Egyptians mummified animals as well as people. Cats were especially *sacred* to the Egyptians. They represented Bast, the cat-headed goddess of happiness. Cats were kept as pets, and when one died, the whole family *shaved* their heads and eyebrows in mourning. Cat mummies were buried with their owners or at the temples of Bast.

Ancient Egyptians also mummified other animals sacred to the gods, such as crocodiles, ibises, and falcons. These animals were

---

动物木乃伊

古埃及人将动物尸体也做成木乃伊。猫对于埃及人来说是神圣的。它们代表贝斯特——代表幸福的猫头女神。猫被当作宠物来养，如果它去世了，全家人要剃光头发和眉毛表示默哀。猫木乃伊和它们的主人葬在一起，或者是葬在贝斯特庙宇。

古埃及人也把其他神圣的动物制成木乃伊，比如鳄鱼、朱鹭、猎鹰。这些动物死后会被送去当作神的祭品。

---

sacred  *adj.* 神圣的                                              shave  *v.* 剃

WORLD MYSTERIES

◆ MUMMIES

sent to the afterlife as offerings to the gods.

Conclusion

Natural mummies have been found around the world. They can be found in the cold, *acidic* water of a marsh in Denmark, in the frozen depths of an Alpine glacier, or in the hot sands of a desert.

The dead have been preserved as mummies by many different cultures, from Buddhist *monks* in Japan to tribesmen in Papua New Guinea. The Incas in Peru, half a world away from the ancient Egyptians, mummified their ancestors in much the same way as the Egyptians. While artificial and natural mummification vary in some ways, they are alike in one important way. All mummification results in the arrest of cell decay, which preserves the body for hundreds, if not thousands, of years.

小结

自然形成的木乃伊在世界各地被发现。他们出现在丹麦冰冷的酸性沼泽中，在阿尔卑斯山的深层冰川中，或者在沙漠的炙热沙子中。

往生者被制成木乃伊的做法源于很多文化的影响，从日本的佛教僧侣到巴布亚新几内亚的部落。距离古埃及人有半个地球之遥的秘鲁的印加人也跟古埃及人用一样的方法埋葬他们的祖先。虽然人工木乃伊和天然的木乃伊有很多不同之处，但他们在重要的一点上是一致的。所有木乃伊的细胞都不会腐败，能使木乃伊完好保存至成百上千年。

acidic *adj.* 酸性的　　　　　　　　　　　　　　　monk *n.* 僧侣

WORLD MYSTERIES

# 6

# Early Birds: Fossils and Feathers

Most of the species of animals that have ever lived on Earth suffer *extinction*. When the conditions of the environment change, such as when the climate cools or the quantity of food decreases, a species may die out if it cannot *adapt to* the new conditions. Paleontologists have learned about a wide variety of such extinct organisms from *fossils*—evidence of *prehistoric* life preserved in rock or other material.

---

## 早期鸟类：化石和羽毛

绝大多数曾经在地球上生活的物种都遭遇过灭顶之灾。当环境条件有所改变，例如气候急剧变冷或是食物数量锐减，不能适应新环境的物种就会灭亡。古生物学家已经从化石中了解到各种各样已经灭绝的生物体，这些化石是留在岩石或其他物质中的史前生命。

---

extinction *n.* 灭绝　　　　　　　　　　adapt to 适应
fossil *n.* 化石　　　　　　　　　　　　prehistoric *adj.* 史前的

◆ **EARLY BIRDS: FOSSILS AND FEATHERS**

**WORLD MYSTERIES**

Some fossils are simple marks that an animal produced while moving, such as footprints or trails left in the ground. Others are hollowed-out impressions of an animal's entire body made in rock. Still others are preserved remains of an animal's body, such as bones or shells.

Fossils show how new kinds of species developed over *eons*. For example, scientists have discovered fossils that lead them to believe that birds developed from reptiles more than 150 million years ago; those reptiles may have been dinosaurs.

Information from Fossils

When the vast majority of animals die, the decomposition activities of bacteria and *fungi* cause their bodies to gradually break down and disappear. However, if conditions are suitable, a dead

---

有些化石是动物活动时所留下的简单痕迹，如脚印或是尾巴印在地上的印记。其他的化石则是在中空的岩石中呈现动物的整个身体。然而也有些只保存着动物一部分身体的残骸，如骨头或外壳等。

化石展示了新物种在亿万年间是如何演变的。例如，科学家已经发现鸟类是一亿五千多万年前从爬行动物演变而来；而那些爬行动物可能是恐龙。

来自化石的信息

绝大多数动物死亡后，细菌和真菌进行分解活动，这导致动物的尸体逐渐分解消失。然而，如果条件适合，动物的尸体会转变成化石，留下它

---

eon *n.* 极漫长的时期；千万年　　　　　　　　　　　　　fungi *n.* 真菌

♦ EARLY BIRDS: FOSSILS AND FEATHERS

animal may transform into a fossil, leaving behind clues about its physical characteristics and how it lived.

Typically, an animal that becomes immortalized as a fossil is buried in *sediment*— such as mud or sand— immediately after it dies. This is more likely to happen in or near rivers, the sea, or other bodies of water. Water that carries minerals, such as calcium, then *soaks* into microscopic spaces inside the bones of the body. As more and more of the bone tissue *dissolves* and decays away, increasing amounts of minerals take the place of the bone. In time, a rocky duplicate of the animal's skeleton is left.

When the body decays completely away, impressions of an animal's body form—showing such features as feathers or scales. All that then remains is the hollow space where the animal's body was, surrounded by sediment.

---

的身体特征及生活方式的线索。

一般情况下，成为不朽化石的动物都是在死亡后立即被如同泥或沙的沉积物所埋葬。这种情况在河流、大海或其他水体附近最可能发生。含有钙或其他矿物质的水会被动物体内骨骼中的微小空间所吸收。随着越来越多骨骼组织的溶解和腐烂，大量的矿物质就会取代骨骼。最终留下一副复制出的岩石骨骼。

当尸体完全腐烂消失后，呈现羽毛或鳞片等特征的动物身体印记便形成了。然后留下来的就只有保存动物尸体的空间，并被沉积物所包围。

---

sediment *n.* 沉淀物  　　　　　　　　　　　soak *v.* 吸收
dissolves *v.* 溶解

## WORLD MYSTERIES

The bones and other characteristics of a fossil tell scientists what the animal looked like. These features also enable scientists to compare the animal with species living today. Similarities and differences between the features in the fossil and those of living organisms may *reveal* how the extinct creature behaved. For example, if the bones in the fossil are similar to bones in bird wings today, maybe the animal was capable of *sustained* flight. Such traits may also indicate that modern birds are related to this extinct animal.

Paleontologists use different *procedures* to determine how old a fossil is—that is, to learn when the animal captured as a fossil lived. Because sediment accumulates year after year, fossils found in deeper sediment are older than fossils in sediment closer to Earth's surface. Scientists obtain their best estimates of a fossil's age by

---

化石中的骨头和其他特征告诉科学家动物的长相。科学家也可以利用这些特征来同现存的物种进行比较。两者之间的相同点和不同点可以展现灭绝动物的行为习惯。例如，如果化石中的骨骼同现代的鸟翼骨骼相似，那么这种动物有能力长时间飞行。这样的特点也可表明现代的鸟类与这种已灭绝的动物有一定关系。

古生物学家运用不同的方法，以确定一块化石的年份———也就是去研究这种被变成化石的动物的存活年代。由于沉积物年复一年的堆积，从深层沉积物中发现的化石会比从接近地表沉积物中发现的化石的年份要久一

---

reveal *v.* 显示　　　　　　　　　　　　　　　　　　　sustain *v.* 保持
procedure *n.* 程序

analyzing certain chemicals in the rock that contains the fossil.

### Prehistoric Birds

Paleontologists have unearthed *numerous* fossils of extinct prehistoric birds. The earliest known bird fossils are of a primitive reptile-like bird called Archaeopteryx, which lived approximately 150 million years ago. These fossils offer compelling evidence that birds descended from reptiles.

### How Old Is That Fossil?

The main chemical technique that paleontologists use to estimate the age of fossils is called radioisotope dating. This method is based on the fact that chemicals called *radioactive isotopes* break down to form other chemicals at a known rate over time. By comparing the

---

些。科学家评估化石年龄的最佳方法是分析化石中所包含的一种特定化学物质。

史前鸟类

古生物学家曾出土了许多灭绝的史前鸟类化石。已知最早的鸟类化石是一种类似原始爬行动物的鸟，叫作始祖鸟，生活在大约一亿五千万年前。这些化石提供了令人信服的证据，表明鸟类是爬行动物的后裔。

那块化石有多少年历史？

古生物学家用来估计化石年龄的主要化学技术叫作放射性同位素年代测定。这种技术的原理是，被称为放射性同位素的化学物质经过一定时间

---

numerous *adj.* 许多的　　　　　　　　　radioactive *adj.* 放射性的
isotope *n.* 同位素

## WORLD MYSTERIES

amount of radioactive isotopes left in a fossil with the amount of their breakdown products, scientists can calculate how long this decay process has been going on. That calculation, in turn, tells scientists how long ago the fossil formed.

The fossils of Archaeopteryx show that this crow-sized animal had some characteristics *resembling* birds and others resembling reptiles. Like modern birds, Archaeopteryx had feathers, wings, and a "wishbone" (a forked bone in the upper chest). However, like a reptile, it had teeth and a long, bony tail. It also had three "fingers" with claws on each wing.

Archaeopteryx probably flew rather poorly. Scientists base that conclusion on the structure of the animal's *sternum* (breastbone) seen

---

的分解后以已知的速度形成其他化学物质。通过对化石中剩下的放射性同位素数量以及放射性同位素分解物的数量进行比较，计算出这一腐化过程持续的时间，进而得知这块化石形成的时间。

始祖鸟的化石表明，这种乌鸦大小的动物有类似鸟类和其他爬行动物的一些特点。同现代鸟类一样，始祖鸟有羽毛、翅膀和一根"叉骨"（在胸腔上部的一根叉状骨头）。然而，它也有像爬行动物一样的牙齿和一条长骨尾巴。它的翅膀上也有长着三根"手指"的爪。

始祖鸟可能飞不高。科学家的结论是从它化石中胸骨的结构得出的。始祖鸟的胸骨呈扁平状。现代鸟类的胸骨有一个突出的部分，在飞行中健

---

resemble *v.* 像；类似于            sternum *n.* 胸骨

◆ EARLY BIRDS: FOSSILS AND FEATHERS

in fossils. The sternum of Archaeopteryx was flat. Modern birds have a sternum with a *protruding* part where robust muscles used in flight are attached. Without such a sternum, Archaeopteryx would have lacked powerful flight muscles.

Paleontologists have discovered several fossils younger than those of Archaeopteryx that *depict* other birds. These fossils reveal how birds developed progressively modern traits over time.

Hesperornis and Ichthyornis were two kinds of *aquatic* birds that lived approximately 90 million years ago. Fossils of Hesperornis show that this bird looked like a large loon, with big webbed feet to assist it in swimming. It also had a beak lined with tiny teeth to enable it to catch fish. However, Hesperornis had only *rudimentary* wing bones, so it could not fly. Ichthyornis resembled a gull, with

---

壮的肌肉会附着于此。如果没有这样的胸骨，始祖鸟就可能缺乏强大的飞行肌。

古生物学家已经发现一些描绘其他鸟类，并比始祖鸟年轻的化石。这些化石揭示了鸟类随着时间的推移而逐步向现代进化的过程。

黄昏鸟和鱼鸟是两种大约生活在九千万年前的水生鸟类。黄昏鸟化石表明这种鸟看上去像一只大潜鸟，游泳时靠脚上的蹼协助。它也有连着小牙齿的鸟喙用来捕鱼。然而，黄昏鸟的翼骨并未长成，所以它不能飞。鱼鸟类似海鸥，有细长且尖的翅膀。它有可能是一种能俯冲入海捕鱼的出色

---

protruding *adj.* 突出的  depict *v.* 描绘
aquatic *adj.* 水中生长的  rudimentary *adj.* 基本的；原始的

WORLD MYSTERIES

◆ EARLY BIRDS: FOSSILS AND FEATHERS

elongated pointed wings. It was probably an excellent flyer that dived into the sea to capture fish.

Fossils prove that many of the main types of birds we know today had developed by about 35 million years ago. These included birds that bore resemblance to modern chickens, doves, ducks, parrots, penguins, owls, and songbirds.

**Birds from Dinosaurs?**

Paleontologists *theorize* that fossils depicting birds with reptile-like characteristics are signs that birds developed from reptiles. Scientists have also *uncovered* fossils of dinosaurs that possessed feathers and other bird-like traits. These fossils provide evidence that dinosaurs were the reptiles from which birds developed.

---

的飞鸟。

化石证明，我们今天所知道的许多主要鸟类已经历了大约三千五百万年的进化历程，其中包括类似现代的鸡、鸭、鸽子、鹦鹉、企鹅、猫头鹰和夜莺等鸟类。

鸟类是从恐龙进化而来？

古生物学家推论说，带有爬行动物特征的鸟类化石有望证明鸟类是由爬行动物进化而来。科学家也发现了拥有羽毛和其他鸟类特征的恐龙化石。这些化石都为鸟类是由恐龙这种爬行动物进化而来提供了证据。

---

theorize  *v.*  推论                                                uncover  *v.*  发现

## WORLD MYSTERIES

Fossils indicate that *carnivorous* dinosaurs called coelurosaurs were like birds in many ways—though scientists classify them as true dinosaurs. The fossils of the most bird-like members of the coelurosaur group are approximately 155 million to 135 million years old. They show that these animals were small for dinosaurs, most ranging in length from 2 to 10 feet (0.6~3 meters). They ran rapidly on two long, *slender* hind legs, which each had four, clawed toes. Their bones were hollow and lightweight. They had sizable eyes. Some even had feathers.

All of these traits are similar to those of birds. Since fossils exhibit these attributes, it's logical to conclude that coelophysis coelurosaurs developed into birds.

One of the coelurosaurs that paleontologists understand best from fossils is Compsognathus. It is known from two well-preserved

---

化石表明，被称作虚骨龙的食肉恐龙在许多方面与鸟类相似——虽然科学家将它归类为真正的恐龙。虚骨龙群中最像鸟类的恐龙化石大约有一亿三千五百万年到一亿五千五百万年的历史。它们都是小型恐龙，体长在2~10英尺（即0.6~3米）。它们都有四只长有脚趾的爪，并能用细长的两条后肢跑得飞快。他们的骨头中空而轻，眼睛却非常大。有些恐龙甚至有羽毛。

所有这些特征都与鸟类相似。凭借化石所展示的这些属性，可以说虚骨龙进化成鸟类这一结论是合乎逻辑的。

古生物学家通过化石了解得最透彻的一种虚骨龙化石便是美颌龙。据

---

carnivorous *adj.* 食肉的        slender *adj.* 纤细的

◆ EARLY BIRDS: FOSSILS AND FEATHERS

fossils, about 145 million years old, which were discovered in Europe.

Compsognathus was one of the smallest dinosaurs that ever lived—some of these creatures were only the size of a chicken. Compsognathus had a long, thin neck and tail and long *hind* legs. On each of its short front legs, it had only two claws—an unusual feature for a dinosaur. Like other coelurosaurs, Compsognathus hunted by running after insects, *lizards*, and other diminutive animals and grabbing them with its razor-sharp claws and teeth.

Scientists know what this dinosaur ate because one of the fossils of Compsognathus includes the remains of its last meal in its stomach. The type of lizard seen in the stomach had extremely long legs, so this lizard must have been a fast runner. Thus, Compsognathus had to be quick to capture this prey.

---

了解，两块从欧洲发现的保存完好的化石约有一亿四千五百万年历史。

美颌龙是有史以来最小的恐龙之一——其中一些动物只有一只鸡的大小。美颌龙有细长的颈、尾和长长的后肢。它每一只短小的前肢上只有两只爪——对恐龙来说这点很不寻常。像其他的虚骨龙一样，美颌龙靠它们锋利的爪子和牙齿追捕昆虫、蜥蜴和其他小动物。

科学家知道这种恐龙的食物，是因为其中一块化石的美颌龙胃里残留着它的最后一餐。这种蜥蜴长有极长的腿，所以它一定跑得很快。因此，美颌龙追捕这猎物时必须迅速。

---

hind *adj.* （动物的腿）后面的　　　　　　　　　lizard *n.* 蜥蜴

## WORLD MYSTERIES

### Fossil Bird in Its Egg

A 121-million-year-old fossil provides evidence that some prehistoric birds—unlike most birds today—could feed themselves immediately after *hatching* from their eggs. The fossil shows the *outline* of an egg with a baby bird still curled up inside. The unhatched bird had a complete set of feathers, strong-looking bones, and a large *skull*. Most birds today are weak and naked when they hatch and must be fed by their parents.

### Conclusion

Much has been learned about prehistoric animal life from fossils. Some of the most fascinating fossils ever uncovered prove that, ages ago, there were creatures that had some characteristics of

---

鸟蛋化石

一个一亿两千一百万年历史的化石证明一些史前鸟类——与现在的鸟类不同——能从孵化后就养活自己。化石显示了一只幼鸟蜷缩在蛋中的轮廓。未孵化的小鸟有着一身完整的羽毛、看起来强壮的骨骼和一个大头盖骨。现今绝大多数鸟类孵化时都比较柔弱并没有羽毛，必须靠它们的父母喂食。

小结

从化石中我们已经了解了许多史前动物的生活。一些曾发现的最令人

---

hatch *v.* 孵出     outline *n.* 轮廓
skull *n.* 颅骨·

◆ EARLY BIRDS: FOSSILS AND FEATHERS

birds and other characteristics of reptiles. Fossils of these organisms lead scientists to theorize that birds developed from dinosaurs.

Dinosaurs *roamed* the Earth for more than 150 million years, but they were unable to adapt when environmental conditions changed about 65 million years ago. According to scientists, Earth's climate may have changed dramatically around that time, perhaps as the result of a *meteorite* impact. Although dinosaurs did not survive this change, birds did. Today, there are more than 9,700 species of birds thriving from the frigid Arctic and Antarctic to the *torrid* tropics.

Some scientists actually classify birds as living dinosaurs. So the next time you see a songbird singing outside your window, might you really be watching and listening to a dinosaur?

---

称奇的化石证明，很久以前，某种生物有着一些类似鸟类和爬行动物的特征。这些生物的化石引导着科学家得出鸟类是由恐龙演化而来的结论。

一亿五千多万年前，恐龙曾漫游于地球，然而，它们没能适应六千五百万年前的环境变化。科学家们认为那个时候可能是由于陨石的撞击，地球气候发生了剧变。恐龙没能逃过这一劫，但是鸟类存活了下来。现在，从寒冷的南北极到酷暑的热带地区，九千七百多种鸟类繁衍昌盛。

实际上，一些科学家已将鸟类归类为活恐龙。所以，下次你看到鸟儿在你窗外高歌时，真的有可能是在注视和聆听一只恐龙哦！

---

roam *v.* 漫游　　　　　　　　　　　　meteorite *n.* 陨石
torrid *adj.* 炎热的

## WORLD MYSTERIES

# 7

# Believe It or Not?

If you heard that *hairy*, smelly giants live in our wilderness, or that *extraterrestrials* make pictures in wheat fields, would you believe it? What if a friend told you an ancient curse causes people to die, or that something in a part of the Atlantic Ocean makes ships and planes disappear? How would you know whether or not these stories were true?

After reading it, you'll have evidence about these four unsolved mysteries. You can decide whether you think they're real or fake.

## 信不信由你

如果你听说有恶臭、长毛的巨人住在荒野里，或是外太空生物在麦田里制造怪圈，你会相信吗？倘若朋友告诉你一个古老的诅咒会置人死地，或是在大西洋某处有东西能使船只和飞机消失呢？你怎么样才能辨别这些故事的真伪？

读过这篇文章之后，你就知道了这四个未解之谜的详细信息。到时，信不信由你。

---

hairy *adj.* 多毛的　　　　　　　　　　extraterrestrial *n.* 外星生物

◆ BELIEVE IT OR NOT?

## WORLD MYSTERIES

### Bigfoot

In remote areas of the pacific Northwest, Native Americans have told stories for hundreds of years of having *encountered* gigantic, *reclusive*, ape-like creatures. The Salish Indians of Canada called them Sasquatch, which means "wild man of the woods," but other tribes use different names. English speakers most often use the name Bigfoot.

In addition to Native Americans, others who have reported encounters with this creature are railway and forest workers, hikers, travelers, and people who live in remote areas. Most of them have never heard the Native American stories, so they haven't had the opportunity to be influenced by other *accounts* of these creatures.

---

大脚野人

几百年来，美洲印第安人一直讲述着在太平洋西北的偏远地区遇到过类猿、隐居的巨大怪物的故事。加拿大的赛利希印第安人称他们萨斯科奇人，意思是"森林中的野人"，但是其他部落有不同的叫法。在英语中，他们通常被称为"大脚野人"。

除了美洲印第安人之外，其他人也声称遇到过这种怪物，目击者包括铁路工人、林业工人、徒步旅行者、游客，还有偏远地区的居民。他们中的大多数人从未听过美洲印第安人有关怪物的故事，因此也无所谓受到那些描述的影响。

---

encounter *v.* 遇到　　　　　　　　　　　　reclusive *adj.* 隐居的
account *n.* 报道

◆ BELIEVE IT OR NOT?

A Bigfoot is reported to be huge, as much as 8 feet (2.5 m) tall, with hair all over its body. Based on the depth of its enormous footprints, its weight is estimated to be between 350 and 800 pounds (160 and 360 kg). People who see one usually report hearing high-pitched screams and smelling a terrible *odor*.

Cryptozoologists (scientists who study hidden animals) and other curious people have spent a great deal of time and money to find out whether Bigfoot really exists. After following up on thousands of eyewitness reports, they have not yet been able to find *proof*.

In 1924, a *lumberjack* named Albert Ostman went into the mountains alone to prospect for gold. During the third night of his trip, he was carried off in his sleeping bag by something huge and smelly. After several hours, it dropped him in a clearing, where four huge, hairy, ape-like creatures surrounded him. They seemed to

---

据称大脚野人体型庞大，有8英尺（2.5米）高，全身都长满了毛。那硕大脚印的深度表明它的体重估计要有350至800磅（160至360公斤）。目击者常说听到野人发出了高亢的尖叫声，还说闻到了一股恶臭味。

未知生物学家（研究未知生物的科学家）和其他好奇的人花费大量时间和金钱来试图查明大脚野人是否真的存在。在追踪了数千个目击者的报道后，他们仍旧没能找到证据。

1924年，一个名叫艾伯特·奥斯曼的伐木工人独自进入大山去淘金。第三晚，他在睡袋中被一个恶臭的大怪物叼走了。几小时之后，他被扔到了一片空地上，睁眼看到四只巨大多毛的类猿怪物包围着他。它们就

---

odor *n.* 气味
lumberjack *n.* 伐木工人

proof *n.* 证据

**WORLD MYSTERIES**

be a family made up of a father, a mother, and two children. Albert escaped, badly shaken but unharmed, after nearly a week. This is just one of many reports of Bigfoot encounters, though not all were so peaceful.

In the vast uninhabited forests and *glaciers* of the northwestern United States, nature quickly gets rid of dead bodies. They decompose or are eaten by insects or other animal scavengers. However, scientists believe that if Bigfoot does exist, someone should be able to find a dead body, a *skeleton*, or fossil remains, yet none has ever been found.

In 1977, a Bigfoot sighting in northern Washington turned out to be a hoax planned by three young men with gorilla suits and walkie-

---

像是由爸爸、妈妈和两个孩子组成的家庭。艾伯特吓得要命，但他并没有受伤，他在大约一周之后逃离了那个地方。这只是遭遇大脚野人的众多故事之一，当然不是所有的故事都是这样有惊无险。

在美国西北部广袤无人的森林和冰川地区，尸体很快就会消失不见。它们或腐烂，或分解，或被昆虫及其他食腐动物吃掉。然而，科学家们相信，如果大脚野人真的存在，就一定会有死尸、骨骼或是化石残骸，但是直到现在什么都没有发现。

1977年，华盛顿北部大脚野人目击事件被揭穿，是三个年轻男子用大猩猩皮毛和步话机设计的骗局。这一事件使人们怀疑，其他报道很有可

---

glacier  *n.*  冰川                                       skeleton  *n.*  骨骼

◆ BELIEVE IT OR NOT?

talkies. This makes people think that other reports must have been faked as well.

## Crop Circles

In fields of tall crops, circles where the plants have been flattened were reported as early as 1590. Farmers thought they were made by wind. In the 1980s, the number of circles increased dramatically, and since then, they have changed from simple circles to complex designs.

Most crop circles form mysteriously in the night, but a few people report having seen them formed by *spaceships* or *whirlwinds*. Sometimes lights are seen in the sky and humming or music is heard, and sometimes radiation can be detected inside the circles. The crops inside circles are not crushed, but instead are bent at the

---

能也是假的。

麦田怪圈

早在1590年就有报道说,在高作物的农田里,植物被打平的地方形成了多个圆圈。农民们认为是风吹所致。20世纪80年代,怪圈的数量显著增加,并且从那时起,它们从简单的圆圈演变成复杂的图案。

很多麦田怪圈在夜晚神秘地形成,但是有人声称自己看到怪圈是由宇宙飞船或旋风造成的。有时候能够在天空中看到光,能听到嗡嗡的响声或是音乐声,有时候在怪圈内部能够探测出辐射。在怪圈里面的作物并没有被压碎,但是作物在茎的最低节点处弯曲。通常这些弯曲的作物比怪圈外

---

spaceship  *n.*  宇宙飞船                    whirlwind  *n.*  旋风

**WORLD MYSTERIES**

◆ BELIEVE IT OR NOT?

lowest node on the stalk. Often these *bent* crops grow better than the unbent plants outside the circle. Scientific experiments suggest that high-powered microwave *beams* might cause the crops to lie down in this way. But from where would they come, and who would be controlling them? Some people think they are messages from beings on other planets.

In areas where many circles are found, people who watch the fields overnight for signs of activity and new circles say that intricate circle patterns can appear in just a few minutes.

Many crop circles are made by humans, for a variety of reasons. Some people just want to prove that it can be done, some people want to play tricks, and others who call themselves "crop artists" say that God inspires them.

---

面不弯曲的作物生长得好。科学实验证明在高能量的微波照射下可能会导致作物如此倒伏。但这种微波从何而来又被谁控制呢？一些人认为，这是外星生命带来的信息。

在那些怪圈大量出现的地方，据在田地中通宵观察活动迹象的人说，精密复杂的怪圈图案在几分钟之内就能出现。

很多麦田怪圈是人为制造的，原因不尽相同。一些人是为了证明怪圈能够做成，一些人在搞恶作剧，还有一些自称为"作物艺术家"的人，说自己得到了上帝的启示。

---

bent *adj.* 弯曲的　　　　　　　　　　　　　　　beam *n.* 光束

WORLD MYSTERIES

In 1991, Englishmen Doug Bower and David Chorley claimed they had made every crop circle since 1978. Some people accepted their explanation of a gigantic hoax. But others doubt they would have the skill and strength to create huge patterns in the dark of night without being seen. Doug *retracted* his confession seven years later and declared that "unknown forces" made the circles.

Some people suggest that the circles are created by *tornadoes*, but crop circle designs are controlled and *intricate*, while a tornado destroys a wide area. Another weather theory is based on an electrically charged whirlwind called a plasma vortex. A plasma vortex can create the strange lights and humming sounds reported

1991年，英国人道格·鲍尔和大卫·乔莱声称从1978年开始是他们制作了每一个麦田怪圈。一些人将他们的弥天大谎信以为真。但是其他人怀疑他们的技术和实力，觉得他们无法在夜晚创作出大量怪圈而且竟然无人知晓。七年后道格收回了他的话，宣布是那些"未知的力量"制作了怪圈。

有人认为怪圈是由龙卷风造成的，但是龙卷风毁坏了大片区域，又怎能收放自如地留下设计精妙的麦田怪圈图案呢？另一个有关天气的说法叫作等离子漩涡，这个气候原理是基于带电旋风现象。麦田怪圈目击者声

retract *v.* 收回          tornado *n.* 龙卷风
intricate *adj.* 复杂的

◆ BELIEVE IT OR NOT?

by crop circle *eyewitnesses*. It can hover in one place or move as if it's under *remote* control, which could make it look like a UFO.

Some researchers have suggested that the U.S. and British military are developing a high-energy weapon powered by microwaves. In this *scenario*, crop circles are produced by test of this top-secret weapon.

The Curse of the Mummy

In 1922, Howard Carter discovered the tomb of the Egyptian pharaoh Tutankhamun, known today as King Tut. The tomb was fulled with incredibly valuable treasures. In 1922, newspapers

---

称看到了怪光，还听到了嗡嗡的响声，这都可能是由等离子漩涡创造的。它能通过远程遥控盘旋在某处或是进行移动，看起来就可能是个不明飞行物。

一些研究人员指出，美国军队和英国军队正在研发一项由微波驱动的高能武器。在研发过程中，怪圈会由这种高绝密武器试射而成。

木乃伊的诅咒

1922年，霍华德·卡特发现了埃及法老图坦卡蒙的墓穴，也就是我们今天说的图坦王。墓里价值连城的宝物多得难以想象。1922年报纸上

---

eyewitness  *n.*  目击者                    remote  *adj.*  遥远的
scenario  *n.*  方案；设想

WORLD MYSTERIES

◆ BELIEVE IT OR NOT?

circulated stories of a curse painted on a tomb wall that said, "They who enter this sacred tomb shall swift be visited by wings of death."

Early Egyptians believed that *cobras* are the protectors of the Pharaohs. On the day Carter opened the tomb, his canary was swallowed by a cobra.

Carter's search for the tomb was funded by Lord Carnarvon. When Lord Carnarvon died in Egypt in 1923, newspaper stories said that he was killed by a pharaoh's curse. It was also said that Carnarvon's dog *howled* and dropped dead in England at the same minute as his owner.

The newspapers reported that 26 people involved with finding the tomb died in the first 10 years. Many of these deaths were supposed to involve *suspicious* circumstances. This mystery has been so

---

流传着写在该墓穴墙壁上的诅咒，内容是："进入此神圣坟墓的人将很快被死神拜访。"

早期埃及人认为眼镜蛇是法老的守护者。在卡特开启坟墓的那一天，他的金丝雀被一只眼镜蛇吞食了。

卡特关于此墓的研究是由卡纳封勋爵提供资金的。1923年，卡纳封勋爵在埃及去世，报纸上说他死于法老的诅咒。据说卡纳封的狗在他去世的同一时间，也开始狂吠并毙死于英格兰。

报纸上说，26个参与发现此墓的人相继在墓穴发现后的10年内去世。大多数人死得很蹊跷。因此，图坦王墓穴与诅咒之谜被用作很多电

---

cobra *n.* 眼镜蛇　　　　　　　　　　　　　　　　howl *v.* 咆哮
suspicious *adj.* 可疑的

## WORLD MYSTERIES

fascinating that it has been used as the theme for many movies, books, and games.

In the early 1900s, reporters sometimes invented facts to make stories more exciting. Lord Carnarvon had actually been sick for 20 years before he died, so the timing of his death might have been just a *coincidence*. Research shows that actually only six people involved with finding the tomb died in the first ten years. Howard Carter worked on the tomb for at least ten years, and yet he lived for 17 years after the discovery, and the curse that was reportedly written in the tomb was not there at all.

It is possible that dead bodies produce bacteria that could cause illness and death. Could this have contributed to Lord Carnarvon's

---

影、书籍和游戏的主题。

20世纪初，记者有时候会虚构事实来使故事更加刺激。事实上，卡纳封勋爵去世前已生病长达20年之久，因此他在发现墓穴后死亡很可能只是巧合。研究表明，事实上发现此墓的人中，只有6人在墓穴发现后10年内死亡。霍华德·卡特从事墓穴研究长达10年，在这一发现后活了17年，所以墓穴内写有咒语的说法完全是无稽之谈。

很有可能是墓中尸体产生的细菌导致人们生病和死亡。这能够解释卡纳封勋爵的死因吗？当今的考古学家戴着橡胶手套，穿着帆布服装来保护

---

coincidence  *n.*  巧合

◆ BELIEVE IT OR NOT?

death? Today's archeologists wear rubber gloves and clothing that protects them, but early people who robbed tombs might have gotten sick in this way. This might have been how stories of a curse got started.

Early Egyptians went to a lot of trouble to prepare their kings for *burial*. They believed that kings should be buried with riches to use in their next life. These Egyptians may have started *legends* of danger to keep people away from the tombs.

Bermuda Triangle

Strange things have been happening to ships and planes for years in an area of the Atlantic Ocean that is generally between Florida, Bermuda, and Puerto Rico. In 1965, Vincent Gaddis wrote a

自己，但早期的盗墓者可能是由于穿戴的衣物而染病了。这可能也解释了诅咒的说法是从何而来的。

　　早期埃及人在筹备法老的葬礼时遇到了很多困难。他们相信，财宝要给法老作为陪葬，供他们来世享用。很可能是这些埃及人最早传播入墓有危险的说法，来使人们远离法老的墓穴。

　　百慕大三角

　　在大西洋某处，船只和飞机上的怪异事件数年来时有发生，这一区域便是由佛罗里达、百慕大群岛和波多黎各构成的三角区。1965年，文森

burial *n.* 埋葬；葬礼　　　　　　　　　　　　legend *n.* 传说

**WORLD MYSTERIES**

◆ BELIEVE IT OR NOT?

book about these strange *occurrences* called Invisible Horizons. He was the first to call the area the Bermuda Triangle, and he also called it the Triangle of Death.

In this area, numerous planes and ships disappear without a trace. Crews mysteriously disappear from ships, dense fogs suddenly appear, and compasses and navigation equipment won't work.

On a clear day in 1945, while a group of planes called Flight 19 was on a routine training mission, all five Avenger *bombers* lost their bearings and disappeared. The rescue airship that went to look for them disappeared as well.

In 1881, the merchant ship Ellen Austin discovered a ghost ship floating without a crew, yet there were no signs of struggle on board.

---

特·盖迪斯写了一本关于这些奇异事件的书，名为《不可见的地平线》。他是第一个把该地区称为"百慕大三角"的人，他也称其为"死亡三角"。

在这一区域，许多飞机和船只消失得踪迹全无。船员突然消失，浓雾突然出现，指南针和导航设备全部失灵。

1945年的一个晴天，美国海军19号机队在执行日常训练任务时，五艘复仇者轰炸机全部失去方向并消失，营救他们的海上飞机也同样消失了。

1881年，艾伦·奥斯丁号商船发现了一艘没有船员的幽灵浮船，然

---

occurrence *n.* 发生的事情　　　　　　　　bomber *n.* 轰炸机

**WORLD MYSTERIES**

A crew boarded to *steer* her to port, but when a thick fog surrounded both ships, they lost contact overnight. When the ghost ship was found the next day, the second crew had disappeared as well.

In 1966, Captain Donald Henry's *tug*, the Good News, was towing a cargo barge from Puerto Rico to Florida. When a dense fog suddenly *swirled* around the barge, the Good News lost the use of all of its instruments and partially lost power. For five minutes the Good News struggled in a tug of war with the fog bank; it finally managed to pull itself and the barge free.

People claim that a mysterious power causes the many losses of ships and crews in the Bermuda Triangle. Because weird lights are

---

而甲板上并没有任何挣扎的痕迹。一组船员登船欲将其靠岸，突然一股浓雾笼罩两艘船，他们整晚都无法与对方取得联系。第二天再发现幽灵船的时候，后来上船的这组船员也消失了。

1966年，唐纳德·亨利船长的拖轮——"好消息"号，从波多黎各拖一艘货船到佛罗里达。突然一团浓雾包围货船，"好消息"号所有仪器都失灵了，部分电源也停止运作。好消息号在雾阵中挣扎了长达5分钟，最终拖船和货船幸免于难。

人们断言是一股神秘的力量使这么多船和船员在百慕大三角神秘消失。因为在那里能看到怪异的光，有人认为是不明飞行物捕获了人类并将

---

steer  *v.*  驾驶　　　　　　　　　　　　　　　　　　　　　tug  *n.*  拖船
swirl  *v.*  快速旋流

◆ BELIEVE IT OR NOT?

seen there, some think that UFOs capture humans and take them away.

Others say the unexplained losses are a result of the *severe* weather common in the area. Hurricanes and violent waterspouts blow up suddenly, and tidal waves are common. Any *vessel* that is destroyed would wash away without a trace. Some of the missing crews, when rescued later, tell stories of being forced to leave their storm-damaged ships.

Some say that nothing unusual is going on in the area. They suggest that some of the losses blamed on the Bermuda Triangle actually happened hundreds of miles away. Other vessels that have been reported lost actually showed up later.

---

他们带走了。

其他人认为这些难以解释的消失是由这一地区常见的恶劣天气导致的。飓风和猛烈的海上龙卷风会突然来袭，海啸也是常有的事。任何已经损坏的船只都会被卷走，踪迹全无。一些船员在失踪后被救，他们讲述了船体破损，被迫弃船的经过。

有人说这里发生的事情没有什么奇怪的。他们表示，人们认为在百慕大三角消失的船只，实际上就消失在数百英里以外。据称已消失的船只很快又出现了。

---

severe *adj.* 严重的 　　　　　　　　　　vessel *n.* 船

# WORLD MYSTERIES

### Conclusion

Mysterious occurrences—things we can't understand—will always exist. Some people will think they are *nonsense*, and others will claim they are real. Now that you've read evidence here about four of them, it's time to *consider* what you've read and determine what you believe. You can use the Internet and the library to find more information. What do you think about these mysteries, and what others can you find?

小结

我们难以理解的神秘事件总是存在。有人认为是无稽之谈,其他人则言之凿凿。现在你已经读到了四个神秘事件的相关信息,可以想想你所读的内容,做出你的判断。你可以利用互联网和图书馆来获得更多的信息。关于这些神秘事件你有什么看法?你还知道其他的神秘事件吗?

---

nonsense *n.* 胡言乱语;蠢话　　　　　　　　　　consider *v.* 思考

◆ THE MYSTERY OF KING TUT

# 8

# The Mystery of King Tut

In 1922, a British archaeologist made a *fantastic* discovery in the country of Egypt. He found the tomb of Tutankhamun, better known as King Tut. Tut ruled ancient Egypt more than 3,300 years ago, becoming pharaoh at the age of nine. He ruled less than a decade before dying suddenly at about age 18. Since the opening of Tut's coffin more than 80 years ago, many have *wondered* how and why the young king died.

Just like detectives, archaeologists try to solve mysteries by

---

## 图坦王之谜

1922年，一位英国考古学家在埃及有一项重大的发现。他发现了图坦卡蒙的坟墓，图坦卡蒙通常被称为"图坦王"。图坦王在3300多年前统治着古埃及，9岁就成了法老。他统治不到10年，就在18岁那年骤然去世了。自从80多年前图坦王的棺材被打开时起，就有很多人在猜想这位年轻的国王过世的经过和原因。

考古学家和侦探一样，通过观察证据和提出问题，尽力解开谜团。图

---

fantastic *adj.* 极大的　　　　　　　　　　wonder *v.* 想知道

**WORLD MYSTERIES**

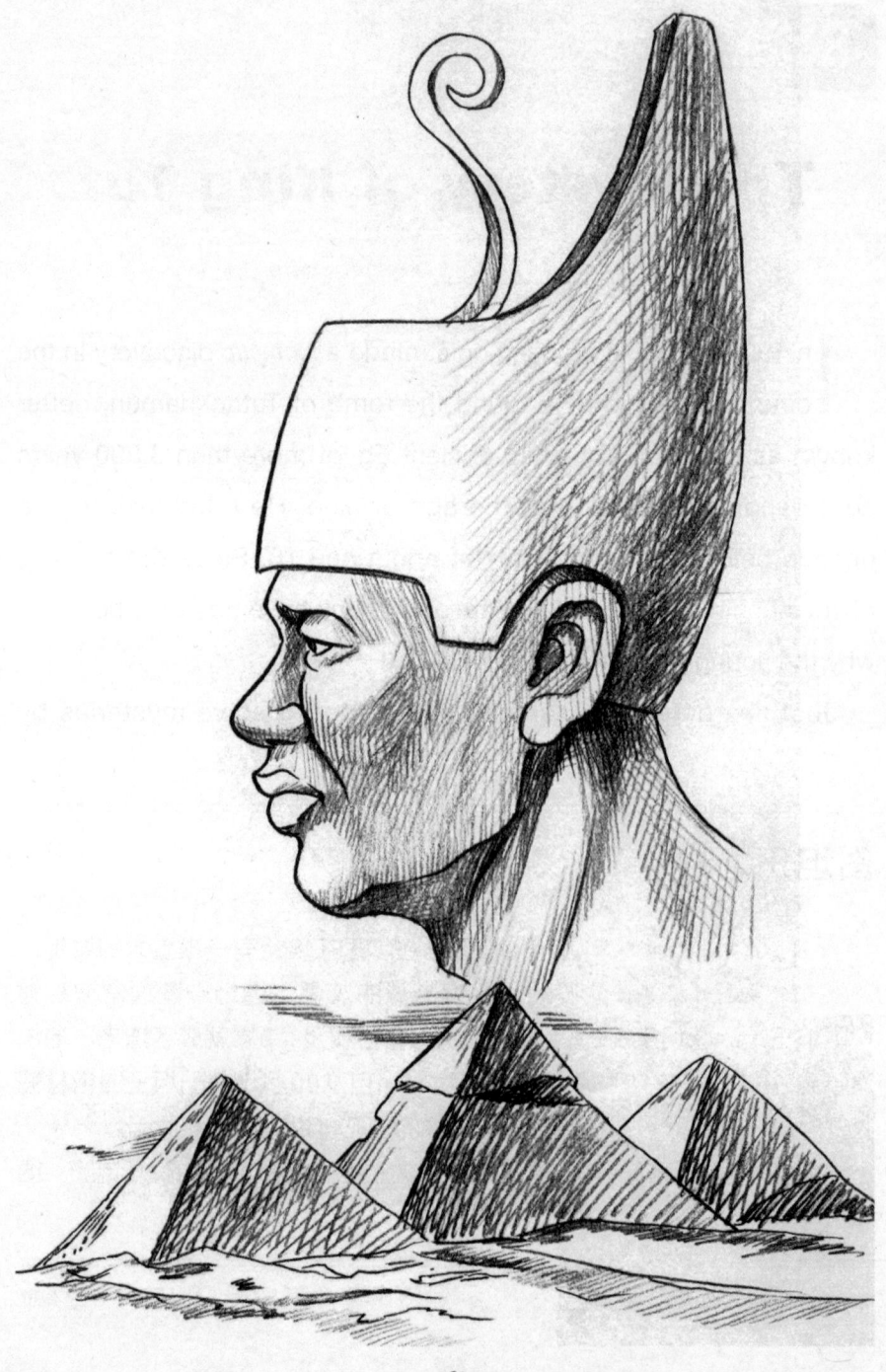

♦ THE MYSTERY OF KING TUT

looking at the evidence and by asking questions. Where did Tut live? What was his life like? Who were his family and friends? Did he have enemies? Answering questions like these may help solve the *ultimate* question: Did King Tut die of natural causes—or was the young pharaoh murdered?

### King Tut's Homeland

Ancient Egypt was ruled for about 3,000 years by a series of 30 *dynasties* (ruling families). Historians group the first 20 dynasties into historical periods called the Early Dynastic Period, the Old Kingdom, the Middle Kingdom, and the New Kingdom.

坦王住在哪？过什么样的生活？他的家人和朋友都是谁？他有没有敌人？回答出诸如此类的问题就可能帮助解决一个终极难题：这位年轻的法老是被谋杀了，还是自然死亡呢？

图坦王的故乡

在长达3000年的时间里，古埃及处于30个朝代（统治家族）的统治之下。历史学家将前20个朝代划分为几个历史阶段，分别叫作"早王朝时期"、"古王国时期"、"中王国时期"和"新王国时期"。

---

ultimate  *adj.* 最终的                   dynasty  *n.* 王朝；朝代

**WORLD MYSTERIES**

King Tutankhamun was a member of the 18th Dynasty, the first ruling family of the New Kingdom, which began around 1540 BC, almost 200 years before Tut was even born.

In ancient Egypt, religious belief was an important part of life. Egyptians at that time *worshiped* many different *deities*—gods and goddesses. To fully understand the mystery surrounding King Tut, one must learn the history behind this religious belief.

Two of Egypt's most important gods at the beginning of the New Kingdom were Ra and Amun. Ra was believed to live within the sun. In images, he was often depicted as a falcon. Amun was usually depicted as a man with a tall crown.

---

　　图坦卡蒙国王是第十八朝的成员，而十八朝是新王国时期的第一代统治家族。新王国时期开始于公元前1540年左右，此后200年，图坦王才降生于世。

　　在古埃及，宗教信仰是人们生活的重要部分。当时的埃及人要敬奉许多神——既有男神，也有女神。要充分理解图坦王的神秘之处，我们就必须了解这些宗教信仰背后的历史。

　　在新王国初期最重要的两个神是"拉"和"阿蒙"。人们相信拉生活在太阳里。他的形象通常是一只猎鹰。而阿蒙的形象则是一个戴着高高的皇冠的人。

---

worship　*v.*　敬奉　　　　　　　　　　　　　　　　　　deity　*n.*　神

◆ THE MYSTERY OF KING TUT

During the early part of the New Kingdom, however, some Egyptians began worshiping the sun in a different way. Instead of seeing the sun as Ra's home, they saw the sun as a god itself. They called this new god Aten and depicted him as a golden *disk* with *rays* of light reaching toward Earth.

As Aten's power as a god grew, other gods such as Ra and Amun were worshipped less and less. But Egypt was still a land of religious freedom, and to most people, this newcomer, Aten, was just another god among many. He did not pose a threat to their religious beliefs until a young man named Amenhotep IV—Tut's father—became pharaoh.

---

然而，在新王国早期，有些埃及人开始用其他的方式敬仰太阳神。他们不再认为太阳是拉的家园，而是认为太阳本身就是神。他们把这位新神称作"阿顿"，并把他的形象描绘成一个发光的金色圆盘，其光线直达地球。

阿顿的神威越来越强，信奉拉与阿蒙的人就越来越少。但是埃及仍然是宗教信仰自由之地，对大多数人来说，这位新神阿顿不过是众多神灵中的一位而已。他并没有威胁到他们的宗教信仰。这种情形一直持续到年轻的阿孟霍特普四世——即图坦王的父亲——成为法老为止。

---

disk *n.* 盘状物                    ray *n.* 光线

## WORLD MYSTERIES

### King Tut's Family

Amenhotep IV began his rule in 1353 BC. He was an odd-looking man with a long face, large lips, and a protruding belly. Amenhotep had been raised in the new Aten religion and was a true believer. He saw Aten as a universal god—a god of all the people in the world, not just Egyptians. The pharaoh believed Aten, the universal sun god, created the world at the beginning of time, ruled over it alone, and continued to give life to the world through his bright rays of light. Thus, Amenhotep IV has been called the world's first monotheist, someone who believes in a single, all-powerful god.

After about five years, the new pharaoh took a *drastic* step. He

---

图坦王的家人

阿孟霍特普四世于公元前1353年开始掌权。他的外貌很奇怪,长脸大嘴,小腹外凸。阿孟霍特普从小信仰的是新神阿顿,并且十分虔诚。他认为阿顿是掌管宇宙的神——不只是埃及人的神,他是全世界人的神。

这位法老相信,是掌管世界的太阳神阿顿最早开辟了天地,并且全权掌管,通过他明亮的光线赐予世上万物以生命。因此,阿孟霍特普四世被称作世界上第一位一神教信徒。一神教信徒指的是只信仰单一的、有无上权力的神灵的人。

大约5年以后,这位新法老采取了激进措施。他发起了一场宗教革

---

drastic *adj.* 剧烈的

◆ THE MYSTERY OF KING TUT

began a religious *revolution*, a sudden and complete change in the official religion of Egypt. He declared that Egyptians could only worship Aten. He changed his name to Akhenaten, which means "He Who Serves Aten." Akhenaten closed and tried to destroy temples that worshiped the other gods.

Akhenaten's actions upset people who were used to worshiping many gods and angered the *priests* of the old gods. Taking away religious freedom sometimes moves people to violence. In various parts of Egypt, people tried to stop the destruction of their *temples*, but the pharaoh's military was able to control them.

In addition to destroying temples, Akhenaten also ordered a new capital city built. He moved the capital away from Thebes and called

命，这是一场突然而彻底的国教变革。他宣布埃及人只能信奉阿顿。他将自己的名字改为"埃赫那顿"，字面意思为"阿顿的仆人"。埃赫那顿关闭、甚至毁掉了供奉其他神灵的多座庙宇。

埃赫那顿的行为激怒了信仰其他神灵的人们，也使得其他教派的牧师们十分恼火。剥夺人们的宗教自由往往会导致暴力行动。在埃及各地，人们都奋力反抗对庙宇的破坏，但是法老的军队最终还是控制了老百姓。

除了毁坏庙宇之外，埃赫那顿还下令建造了一个新城作为首都。他将首都从底比斯迁移到新城，并将新城命名为"埃赫塔顿"，字面意思是

revolution *n.* 革命
temple *n.* 寺庙

priest *n.* 牧师；神父

**WORLD MYSTERIES**

the new city Akhetaten, which means "Horizon of Aten." Today this area is called Amarna, and Akhenaten's revolution is called the Amarna Revolution.

Many people remained angry throughout Akhenaten's *reign* and perhaps through the reign of his son. Due to the drastic religious changes *initiated* by his father, Tut inherited enemies. His father's revolutionary actions undoubtedly created some of the mystery surrounding the reign and death of King Tut.

But was anyone angry enough to commit murder?

It was in this new capital of Egypt that King Tut was born in about 1342 BC. No one knows for sure who his parents were, but most

---

"阿顿的视线"。今天这座城市已更名为"阿马尔奈",而埃赫那顿的革命又称作"阿马尔奈变革"。

许多人还是对埃赫那顿的统治深表不满,而且一直把怨气延续他儿子身上。由于图坦的父亲发起的激烈的宗教变革,很多人将图坦视为敌人。毫无疑问,他父亲的变革行动也是造成图坦王统治期间及去世后的谜团中的重要促因。

但是,是否真正有人出于愤怒而实施了谋杀呢?

公元前1342年,图坦王出生在埃及的这座新都。没有人知道他的父母是谁,但大多数历史学家认为他的父亲是埃赫那顿,他的母亲是埃赫那

---

reign  *n.*  统治时期　　　　　　　　　　　　　initiate  *v.*  发起

◆ THE MYSTERY OF KING TUT

historians feel his father was Akhenaten and his mother was Lady Kiya, one of Akhenaten's wives. The boy was named Tutankhaten, meaning "the Living Image of Aten."

Akhenaten died in 1336 BC after 17 years of rule. What happened next is as *puzzling* as who Tut's parents were. There were apparently two rulers who had very brief reigns after Akhenaten's death.

One of them may have been a brother of Tutankhaten. The other may have been a queen named Nefertiti. No one knows for sure. In any case, three or four years after Akhenaten's death, the *throne* of Egypt was again empty so nine-year-old Tutankhaten became pharaoh.

---

顿的妻子之一——奇娅王后。图坦王出生时名字是"图坦卡顿",意思是"阿顿的形象"。

埃赫那顿在统治埃及17年之后于公元前1336年去世。接下来发生的事情,就如同图坦父母的身份谜团一样难以探寻真相。在埃赫那顿去世后,显然有两位统治者在短期内统治过埃及。

一位可能是图坦卡顿的哥哥,另一位是奈费尔提蒂女王。没有人知道到底发生了什么。总之,埃赫那顿去世三四年之后,埃及的国王宝座再次空出,所以九岁的图坦卡蒙成为法老。

---

puzzling *adj.* 令人迷惑不解的　　　　　　　　throne *n.* 王位

## WORLD MYSTERIES

### Queen Nefertiti

Except for Cleopatra, no other queen of Egypt is as well known as Nefertiti. She was the favorite wife of Pharaoh Akhenaten. Nefertiti became the *stepmother* of the young Prince Tutankhaten (later Tutankhamun) when his mother died. Nefertiti died in her early 30s.

### The Boy Pharaoh

Before and during his reign, Tut lived the life of the *wealthy*. He wore jewelry, linen clothes, perfumed oils, and makeup. Archaeologists found all these items in his tomb. He would have been expected to hunt, usually with a bow and from a chariot, and

---

奈费尔提蒂女王

除了克利奥帕特拉，埃及最有名的女王就是奈费尔提蒂女王了。她是埃赫那顿法老最喜欢的王妃。在小王子图坦卡顿（后来改为"图坦卡蒙"）母亲过世后，她就成了小王子的继母。奈费尔提蒂30岁出头便过世了。

年轻的法老

图坦在掌权前和掌权时，一直过着富足的生活。他戴着珠宝，穿亚麻衣服，喷香水，并且化妆。考古学家在他的坟墓里发现了这些用品。他也可能带着弓箭、驾着战车去打猎，或者像别的孩子一样玩着游戏度过童

---

stepmother *n.* 继母        wealthy *adj.* 富有的

◆ THE MYSTERY OF KING TUT

he might have otherwise passed the time playing games as children do everywhere. Chariots, nearly 50 *bows*, and senet (a board game) were placed in his tomb for his use in the afterlife.

During his reign, Tutankhaten married his half-sister Ankhesenpaaten, a daughter of Nefertiti. Ankhesenpaaten's name means "She Lives Through Aten." Marriages between close *relatives* were common in Egyptian royal families so the family could keep their lands and the power that came with them. The couple had two children, but neither lived.

King Tut had several servants in the court. One personal attendant, Tutu, had served Tut's family for years, since his grandfather had been king. Other servants, some even younger than

年。他的坟墓里有多辆战车、近50张弓还有塞尼特棋（一种棋盘游戏），以供来生使用。

图坦卡顿掌权期间，娶了奈费尔提蒂的一个女儿、也是他的同父异母妹妹安克姗海帕顿为妻。安克姗海帕顿名字的意思是"她为了阿顿而活着"。在埃及的皇室家族中，近亲结婚很常见，这样整个家族就可以一直拥有他们与生俱来的土地与权利。这对夫妻有过两个孩子，但都不幸夭折。

图坦王在宫廷里有几个仆人。有一位贴身仆人叫图图，从图坦的祖父掌权时起，图图已侍奉图坦家族多年。其他的仆人，包括比图坦王年龄还

bow *n.* 弓  relative *n.* 亲属

## WORLD MYSTERIES

King Tut, would help him with even the smallest *tasks*. For example, he had a cup bearer, whose job was to make sure everyone's drinking cups stayed full, especially the young king's.

Because the pharaoh was so young, the *military* and political work of the royal court was mostly carried out by others—two men in particular. One of them was an aging military officer and adviser named Ay. The other was a great army general named Horemheb. Although they had both served Akhenaten, they strongly disliked his religious reforms. The two hoped King Tut would bring back the old ways of worshiping.

Horemheb and Ay wanted Tut to end the worship of Aten. They especially wanted Tut to return Amun to his former glory as chief

---

小的仆人，会帮他做所有事情，无微不至。比如说，他有一个茶水管家，专门负责随时为大家添茶倒水，特别是要侍奉好年轻的国王。

　　因为法老的年龄太小，皇室的军事及政治公务大多是由其他人完成的——最突出的有两个人。一位是年事已高的军队长官和参谋阿伊。另一位是军队的大将军霍伦海布。尽管他们都效忠于埃赫那顿，但是他们都很不喜欢他的宗教改革。两人都希望图坦王可以使国家恢复旧日的宗教信仰自由。

　　霍伦海布和阿伊希望图坦王能够不再崇拜阿顿。他们特别希望图坦王可以将阿蒙重新指定为主要的供奉神。图坦王对此言听计从，并且把名字

---

task *n.* 任务　　　　　　　　　　　　　　　military *adj.* 军事的

◆ THE MYSTERY OF KING TUT

god. The king did so, and changed his name from Tutankhaten to Tutankhamun, "the Living Image of Amun." The queen also took a new name, Ankhesenamun. Historians are certain that Ay and Horemheb were the main forces behind the changes that took place during King Tut's reign. Because he was so young, they believe the pharaoh did as he was told.

As part of a return to the old ways, the royal court moved back to Thebes. The once thriving city of Amarna, *devoted to* the god Aten, was left to decay in the Egyptian sun.

从"图坦卡顿"改为"图坦卡蒙",意思为"阿蒙的形象"。女王也改了名字,叫"安克姗海娜蒙"。历史学家确定霍伦海布和阿伊两个人是图坦王掌权期间进行宗教变革的主要幕后力量。因为法老年纪太小,他们认为法老只是听他们的话行事而已。

作为回归旧日风格的一种表现,皇室家庭又迁回了底比斯。为信奉阿顿神而建造的阿马尔奈,盛极一时,现在在埃及的阳光下逐日衰败下去。

devote to  为……做贡献

**WORLD MYSTERIES**

### End of a Dynasty

In 1322 BC, when he was about 18 years old, King Tutankhamun died. How he died was not *recorded* and remains a mystery. The young pharaoh was mummified and then buried in a tomb in the Valley of the Kings, a large royal *cemetery* near the city of Thebes.

Because Tut had no living children, the throne of Egypt was open to someone who was not a member of the royal family. Ay, because of his long experience in the court, became the new pharaoh and married Tut's widow. After ruling for just four years, Ay died in 1319 BC. Horemheb then became pharaoh.

---

一个王朝的终结

公元前1322年，图坦卡蒙18岁的时候骤然暴亡。他究竟为什么暴亡没有留下记录，到现在也还是个谜。这位年轻的法老被做成木乃伊，然后埋在帝王谷的一座墓穴里。帝王谷是在底比斯城内的一处很大的皇家墓地。

因为图坦王没有子嗣，埃及的皇位就要传给非皇室的成员。阿伊因为在皇室中多年的工作经验，成为新的法老，并与图坦王的遗孀结婚。阿伊统治埃及仅仅4年，就于前1319年去世了。然后霍伦海布成为法老。

---

record *v.* 记录                    cemetery *n.* 墓地

◆ THE MYSTERY OF KING TUT

To show his devotion to Amun, Horemheb ordered the destruction of everything connected with the Aten religion and Akhenaten. In Amarna, his men *demolished* the abandoned temples of Aten. They also *smashed* statues of Akhenaten and his family—including King Tut—and gouged their names and faces from wall art. Later, workers removed the blocks of stone with the wall art from the buildings in the city and used them for construction projects in Hermopolis, a city on the other side of the Nile River near Amarna.

Horemheb ruled for 27 years, dying in 1292 BC. With his death, the 18th Dynasty ended. Later, Ramses II, a great pharaoh of the 19th Dynasty who had served with Horemheb in the Egyptian army, completed the destruction of Amarna. The shattered *remnants* of

霍伦海布为了表达对阿蒙的忠心，下令毁掉一切和阿顿教及埃赫那顿有关的东西。在阿马尔奈，他手下的人拆毁了阿顿教废弃的神庙。他们还砸碎了埃赫那顿及其家人的雕像——包括图坦王的雕像——还从墙上凿下了他们的名字和画像。后来，工人们把城里楼体上的石砖都拆了下来，砖上还有壁画，这些砖后来用于阿马尔奈附近、尼罗河畔的赫尔莫波利斯城的建筑工程。

霍伦海布统治埃及27年，于公元前1292年去世。他的去世也标志着第十八个王朝的终结。后来，曾在埃及军队里跟随霍伦海布的拉美西斯二世

---

demolish *v.* 彻底摧毁      smash *v.* 打碎；破碎
remnant *n.* 残余

**WORLD MYSTERIES**

♦ THE MYSTERY OF KING TUT

Akhenaten's once-splendid capital were covered by drifting sand and forgotten.

King Tut's Tomb

In the 1800s, many archaeologists went to Egypt to study Egyptian picture writing, called *hieroglyphics*, on walls and monuments. From the writing, archaeologists learned a lot about the pharaohs of Egypt. They learned that the tombs of pharaohs would be filled with all the things a person might need in the afterlife. Expecting to find riches, they found the pharaohs' tombs, but were disappointed. Every tomb had been robbed of its valuable treasures by thieves long ago. By the early 1900s, archaeologists believed

成为第十九个王朝的一位伟大的法老。他掌权期间完成了对阿马尔奈城的毁坏工作。一度繁华的埃赫塔顿现在只剩下零星的废墟，并被世人所遗忘。

图坦王的墓穴

19世纪，许多考古学家来到埃及，研究埃及墙壁上和纪念碑上的图画式文字，这种文字叫作"象形文字"。从象形文字中，考古学家知道了很多关于埃及法老们的事情。他们知道了法老们的墓穴里会放满他们来生可能用到的东西。他们期望在法老们的墓穴中发现一些财富，却失望而归。每间墓穴中的珍宝在很久以前就被盗贼洗劫一空了。到20世纪初，考

hieroglyphic  n.  象形文字

WORLD MYSTERIES

they had discovered the tomb of every known pharaoh except one: Tutankhamun.

A British archaeologist, Howard Carter, was determined to find it. Carter searched for Tut's tomb for more than five years with no success. In 1922, he persuaded the man paying for the search, Lord Carnarvon, to pay him for one more season.

Luckily for the world, his *persistence* paid off. Later that year, Carter found Tut's tomb in almost undisturbed condition. It contained a wealth of *artifacts*, including thrones, jewelry, weapons, and statues. The mummy of Tutankhamun, covered with a large gold mask, lay within three nested coffins. The innermost coffin was made of about 242 pounds (110 kilograms) of pure gold. Carter's discovery created

古学家们认定他们几乎发现了每一个已知的法老的墓穴，只有一个没有找到：就是图坦卡蒙的墓穴。

英国的考古学家霍华德·卡特决心要找到这座墓穴。他花了5年多的时间寻找却一无所获。1922年，他说服了为探索活动提供资金的卡纳封勋爵，请他再提供一个季节的探索资金。

天大的好运降临在他的头上，他的坚持终于得到了回报。那年的晚些时候，卡特在一个几乎完全隐蔽的地方发现了图坦王的墓穴。墓穴内有无数的奇珍异宝，包括皇冠、珠宝、武器和雕像。图坦卡蒙的木乃伊盖着很大的金色面罩，躺在一个三层的棺材中。最里层的棺材是用242磅（110

persistence *n.* 坚持不懈     artifact *n.* 手工艺品

◆ THE MYSTERY OF KING TUT

a *sensation*, and Tut became the most famous pharaoh in history.

### The Mummy's Curse

In November 1922, Lord Carnarvon attended the opening of Tut's tomb. A few months later, he died from an infected mosquito bite. Soon after that, two other people who had entered the tomb died *prematurely*. These deaths gave rise to the legend of "The Mummy's Curse." The legend said that anyone who dared to disturb Tut's resting place was *doomed*. However, most people associated with the tomb were not affected by the curse. In fact, Howard Carter, a real life Indiana Jones, the man who should have been the most cursed of all, lived until the age of 66.

---

公斤）纯金打造的。卡特的发现引起了轰动，图坦也成为历史上最有名的法老。

木乃伊的咒语

1922年11月，卡纳封勋爵参加了图坦王墓穴的开墓仪式。几个月后，他就因被染病的蚊虫叮咬而死亡。此后不久，另外两个进入过墓穴的人也突然死亡。这三起死亡引起了"木乃伊的咒语"的说法。人们传说任何敢打扰图坦王安息的人都会被诅咒。但是，大部分与墓穴有联系的人并未被诅咒。实际上，最应该受到诅咒的现实版"夺宝奇兵"——霍华德·卡特——到66岁才与世长辞。

---

sensation *n.* 轰动　　　　　　　　prematurely *adv.* 过早地
doom *v.* 注定

## WORLD MYSTERIES

### The Suspects

Early death was nothing unusual in ancient times. The average life *span* in ancient Egypt was about 30 years, and many people didn't live that long. Still, there is plenty of reason to believe that King Tut, at about the age of 18, may have been the *victim* of murder. Several people had reasons to kill him.

Ay and Horemheb, who controlled many of King Tut's decisions, both became pharaohs after Tut's death. Perhaps they longed for the throne while Tut was alive. They must have been tempted by the fact that there was no *heir* to the throne. Thus, if they wanted to seize power, the time to do it was before Tut had children who lived, or before he reached adulthood and pushed the two men aside. Some archaeologists say that Ay and Horemheb may have joined forces to kill Tut, perhaps with poison.

---

嫌疑人

早亡在古代并非奇怪之事。古埃及人的平均寿命约为30岁，有很多人不到这个年纪就去世了。但是还是有充分理由相信，18岁暴亡的图坦王可能是被谋杀致死的。有杀人动机的可能有这几个人。

阿伊和霍伦海布控制着图坦王的许多决策，在图坦王死后，二人都成为埃及的法老。可能他们在图坦王在世的时候就觊觎法老的宝座了。他们谋杀的动机可能还有图坦王没有子嗣可以继承王位。这样，如果他们想要掌权的话，就要在图坦王有孩子之前动手，不然等他长大了就会把这两人推到一边。有些考古学家说阿伊和霍伦海布可能加入了杀害图坦王的行动中，很可能使用了毒药。

---

span *n.* 时间段      victim *n.* 受害者
heir *n.* 继承人

◆ THE MYSTERY OF KING TUT

Ay and Horemheb are the most likely suspects, but they are not the only ones. Some researchers have identified two of Tut's servants as possible murderers: the cupbearer and his personal attendant, Tutu. They were among the very few people *permitted* to enter the king's bedroom. Either man could have murdered the pharaoh, perhaps by striking his head with a heavy object while he slept.

Horemheb included an inscription on a statue of himself, found in his tomb, that claims he is *innocent* of Tut's death. Even though he destroyed the city that Tut's father built, Horemheb insists he always served the young pharaoh faithfully, then warns, "Egyptian brothers, don't ever forget what foreigners did to our King Tutankhamun." This note points to a foreigner.

---

阿伊和霍伦海布是嫌疑最大的人，但他们并不是唯一有谋杀可能的人。有些调查者认为图坦王的两个仆人可能是谋杀犯：即茶水仆人和他的贴身仆人图图。很少有人能够进入国王的寝宫，但这两个人可以。两个人都有嫌疑谋杀了法老，可能是在法老入睡时用重物敲击了他的头部。

在霍伦海布的墓穴中，霍伦海布在自己的雕像上刻了一行字，声明他与图坦王的死无关。尽管是他毁掉了图坦王的父亲建造的城市，但他坚持说他始终忠心耿耿地服侍这位年轻的法老。他还警告说："埃及的弟兄们，不要忘记了外国人对我们的图坦卡蒙国王做了什么。"这句话把矛头指向了外国人。

---

permit *v.* 允许　　　　　　　　　　　　innocent *adj.* 无辜的

## WORLD MYSTERIES

The servant Tutu was of foreign origin, and he was said to be a rather suspicious character. A group of *amateur* archaeologists in Egypt contends that Tutu was *spying* for an Egyptian vassal state, a country conquered and then ruled by Egypt. They think Tutu could have murdered both Tut and Akhenaten when they discovered what he was doing.

### The Body

For many years, people have theorized that Tut was indeed killed by a blow to the head. They based that belief on X-ray studies of the pharaoh's mummy made in 1968 and in 1978. The *X-rays* showed

---

仆人图图有外国血统，并且据说性格多疑。埃及一组业余的考古人员坚持认为，图图是埃及的一个附属国派来的间谍，附属国是指被埃及征服并统治的国家。他们认为图坦王和埃赫那顿可能都是被图图谋杀的，因为他们发现了他的身份。

尸体

多年来，人们始终相信图坦王是头部被击致死的。这一说法是基于1968年和1978年对法老的木乃伊进行X光检查得出的。X光片显示图坦王

---

amateur *n.* 业余爱好者      spy *v.* 从事间谍活动
X-ray *n.* X光

damage to the back of Tut's skull. Experts said the damage was strong evidence that Tut had been hit on the back of the head with a heavy object. But was that really true?

In 2005, researchers in Cairo, Egypt, decided to answer the question once and for all. The group was led by a top Egyptian archaeologist, Zahi Hawass. The researchers studied King Tut's mummy with an *advanced* X-ray technique called CT (CAT) scanning. A CT scanner takes numerous X-rays of an object from different angles. The X-ray information is fed to a computer, which uses the

---

的后颅骨受过伤。专家们认为这一伤痕是证明图坦王头部受到重物击打的有力证据。但是真的是这样吗？

2005年，埃及开罗的研究者们决定找到问题真正的答案。这群研究者由一位顶尖的埃及考古学家札希·哈瓦斯领队。研究者们用先进的X光技术研究了图坦王木乃伊，这种技术也叫CT（或CAT）扫描。一次CT扫描需要对一个物体进行不同角度的X光拍照。X光信息会传到电脑里，电脑

---

advanced *adj.* 先进的

## WORLD MYSTERIES

information to produce images. CT images are much more detailed than ones made with *regular* X-ray machines.

Hawass announced that King Tutankhamun *definitely* did not die from a blow to the head. He said the skull damage, revealed by the earlier X-ray studies, had been caused in other ways, after Tut's death. In fact, the injuries may have happened during mummification when King Tut was embalmed.

The mystery doesn't stop there. The researchers did find new evidence of what might have killed Tut. The CT scans showed that the king had suffered a broken leg. Hawass said the boy may have developed an infection from the injury and died a few days later.

---

利用这些信息来形成图像。CT图像比普通X光机形成的图像要具体得多。

哈瓦斯宣称图坦卡蒙国王绝对不是死于头部受击。他说之前的X光研究表明，颅骨的伤痕是图坦王去世后因为其他的原因造成的。实际上，那些伤痕可能是在将国王制作成木乃伊的过程中造成的。

这个谜还没有结束。研究者们确实发现了可能使图坦王致死的新证据。CT扫描显示这位国王的腿部受过伤。哈瓦斯说可能是伤口感染，导致年轻的图坦王数日后死亡的。

---

regular *adj.* 普通的        definitely *adv.* 一定地；确定地

### THE MYSTERY OF KING TUT

**Mystery Solved?**

So, is that the end of the mystery? Maybe not. Some members of Hawass's group said the broken leg might have also happened when Tut was being embalmed. Others felt certain that Howard Carter's team caused the break when they removed Tut's body from it's inner coffin. However, Hawass agreed that it's still possible that Tut was poisoned. But if that's what happened, we'll probably never find proof of it, much less find out who did it. *Needless* to say, there were many people who had *motives* for murder. Thus, the mystery surrounding King Tut's death continues. We may never know what really happened.

谜团已解？

那么，这个谜到此为止了吗？也许还没完。哈瓦斯小组的一些成员认为腿伤也可能是在制作图坦王的木乃伊时形成的。还有人确定是霍华德·卡特小组的人在将图坦王的尸体搬出最里层的棺材时造成了伤痕。不管怎样，哈瓦斯仍然同意图坦王可能是被毒死的。但是如果真是这样的话，我们可能永远找不到相关证据，更别说要找到凶手了。显而易见，很多人都有谋杀的动机。因此，图坦王的死亡之谜仍在继续。我们可能永远无法得知真相。

needless *adj.* 不必要的        motive *n.* 动机

## WORLD MYSTERIES

# 9

# Prehistoric Giants

Imagine traveling in a time machine to walk through a forest millions of years ago. As you *stroll* along, you suddenly hear a loud snorting behind you. When you turn, you see a huge animal, bigger than a house! You may think at first that this giant is a dinosaur—but it might not be.

Many prehistoric animals other than dinosaurs were giants. There

---

## 史前巨型动物

想象一下通过时光机行走在数百万年前的森林里,当你漫步其中时,突然听到背后有巨大的鼾声,你转身的时候看到一个巨型动物,比一栋房子还要大!首先你可能想到的是恐龙,但或许并不是。

除了恐龙之外,还有许多史前动物体型巨大。这里有巨型爬行动物以

---

stroll  v. 散步

◆ PREHISTORIC GIANTS

**WORLD MYSTERIES**

were other giant reptiles as well as giant species of shellfish, insects, *centipedes*, fish, amphibians, birds, and mammals. There was even a giant ape, almost like King Kong!

Scientists called *paleontologists* learn about prehistoric animals from shells, footprints, and fossils (remains or traces of animals, such as bones). Paleontologists can use a fossil to learn when and where an animal lived, how big it was, what kind of food it ate, and how it moved. Sometimes, paleontologists can even *remove* DNA from animal remains. Tests of this DNA can show how the prehistoric animal is related to animals living today.

---

及巨型贝壳类动物、昆虫、蜈蚣、鱼、两栖动物、鸟类以及哺乳动物。甚至会有巨型类人猿，形似金刚！

古生物学家们从贝壳、脚印以及（动物留下的诸如骨头的遗迹和痕迹的）化石中研究史前动物。通过化石，古生物学家能够了解到它们存活的时期和地点、它们的体型、食物以及它们是如何行动的。有时，古生物学家甚至可以从其动物残骸中提取DNA，通过史前动物DNA的检测可以探究它们和现存动物之间的联系。

---

centipede *n.* 蜈蚣　　　　　　　　　paleontologist *n.* 古生物学者
remove *v.* 取走

◆ PREHISTORIC GIANTS

Scientists *divide* Earth's history into several different periods of time. These periods are grouped into different *eras*. As you read this book, pay special attention to parts that discuss causes and effects of various events, such as why a species disappeared during a certain period.

Enjoy your prehistoric journey with giants!

Giant Invertebrates

Set your time machine for the Paleozoic era to see some giant invertebrates (animals without backbones). Some fly through the air, and others swim in the oceans, so don't forget to bring your swimsuit!

---

科学家把地球历史划分为代，代下面划分不同的纪。当你读这本书的时候，读到有关多个事件因果关系的部分要尤为注意。比如，为什么一个物种会在某一特定时期消失。

希望你会喜欢这次和巨型动物的史前之旅！

巨型无脊椎动物

我们跟随时光机到古生代来看一些巨型无脊椎动物（没有脊柱的动物），它们有些可以在天空飞翔，有些能够在海中遨游，所以开始此次旅行时不要忘记带泳衣哟！

---

divide *v.* 划分　　　　　　　　　　　　　　era *n.* 时代

WORLD MYSTERIES

### Cameroceras—Scariest Shellfish

It is 470 million to 440 million years ago, and all animals live in the ocean. What are you waiting for? *Dive* in to see Cameroceras, a giant squidlike shellfish. Its head and eight *tentacles* stick out of a cone-shaped shell, which might grow as long as 36 feet (11 m). Cameroceras swims by forcing water out of its shell through a tube. The force of the water makes the animal move in the opposite direction. This is similar to a balloon releasing air and fluid across the room.

Cameroceras hunts *trilobites* and other sea animals. It *grabs* these animals with its tentacles and uses its sharp beak to tear them to pieces.

---

鹦鹉螺——最可怕的贝壳类动物

四亿七千万年到四亿四千万年前，所有动物都生活在海洋中。你还等什么？潜入水中，看看这种乌贼状的巨型贝壳类生物吧。它的头和八个触须从锥形壳中伸出，长度可长达36英尺（11米）。它通过一条管子将壳内水分挤压出来，就能够游动。水的阻力使它向相反的方向游动，这和气球被放气时便会在屋内飞行的原理类似。

鹦鹉螺捕捉三叶虫和其他海洋动物为生，它用触须抓住这些动物，再用利嘴把它们撕成碎片。

---

dive *v.* 潜水　　　　　　　　　　　　　　　　tentacle *n.* 触角
trilobite *n.* 三叶虫　　　　　　　　　　　　　grab *v.* 抓

◆ PREHISTORIC GIANTS

## Meganeura—Dangerous Dragonfly

If you travel more than 100 million years after Cameroceras roamed the seas, you will probably end up in a *swampy* forest, about 311 million to 282 million years ago. And you might want to duck, because a giant dragonflg is *swooping* down through the tropical air. Meganeura is bigger than most birds you know. It has a wingspan of 2.5 feet (76 cm), making it the largest insect ever known.

You've probably noticed that the air is heavier than you're used to. That's because there's more oxygen in it. This heavy air helps

---

巨蜻蜓————一种危险的蜻蜓

如果你漫步在鹦鹉螺出现的一亿年之后，你或许会闯入距今三亿一千一百万年至2亿8200万年的沼泽森林中。在那里有一种大型蜻蜓在空中横冲直撞，可能会使你想要躲进水中。巨蜻蜓比你所要知道的鸟类都要大。它有长达2.5英尺（76厘米）的翅膀，是现今已知最大的昆虫。

你或许已经注意到，这里的空气比几亿年后的今天更重，这是因为空气中有更多氧气。较重的空气可以支撑住巨蜻蜓身体的重量，而剩余的氧

---

swampy *adj.* 沼泽的　　　　　　　　　　　　　　　　swoop *v.* 飞扑

## WORLD MYSTERIES

support the weight of the Meganeura, and the extra oxygen allows Meganeura to grow to a giant size.

### Arthropleura—Biggest Bug

Now that Meganeura has flown by, crawling toward you along the forest floor is Arthropleura , the largest land *arthropod* ever. But it isn't a six-legged insect. It is more like a 60-legged centipede, and it can grow longer than 8 feet (2.5 m). It lives in swampy forests between 340 million and 280 million years ago. Like Meganeura, Arthropleura grows so large because the air is heavy with oxygen.

---

气则使得巨蜻蜓长出巨大的身型。

古蜈蚣虫——最大的虫类

现在巨蜻蜓已经飞走，森林地面上朝你爬过来的是古蜈蚣虫——现今最大的陆地节肢动物。然而它不是六条腿的昆虫，它更像是60条腿的蜈蚣。体长可达8英尺（2.5米），它生活在三亿四千万年到二亿八千万年前的沼泽森林中。像巨蜻蜓一样，由于空气中氧气多，密度大，所以古蜈蚣虫的体型也很大。

---

arthropod *n.* 节肢动物

## Giant Fish and Amphibians

The next giants you will visit on your journey through time are a fish and an amphibian who live during different periods of the Mesozoic era. You might want to bring your *snorkel* as you head out to sea.

### Leedsichthys—Largest Fish

Leedsichthys is no "big fish that got away" story. It is real. The largest fish that ever lived, it can grow almost 90 feet (27.5 m) long in the seas of 165 million to 155 million years ago.

Leedsichthys *gulps* in huge mouthfuls of water as it swims. At the back of the fish's mouth are more than 40,000 long, thin teeth. These

---

巨型鱼类和两栖动物

接下来你将要观赏到的是生存在中生代不同时期的鱼和两栖动物,当你潜入海中的时候,你可能会想要带呼吸管了。

利兹鱼——最大的鱼

利兹鱼不是编入本书的"大鱼"。然而它确实是有史以来最大的鱼。它生活在一亿六千五百万年到一亿五千五百万年前,身长可达90英尺(27.5米)。

利兹鱼游泳的时候会大口吞水,在它的口腔后部是4万颗又长又尖的牙齿。在它把水喷出时,这些牙齿就像筛子一样把虾类、水母及其他小型

---

snorkel *n.* 水下通气管　　　　　　　　　　　　gulp *v.* 急吞

## WORLD MYSTERIES

teeth act like a *screen* to keep in shrimp, jellyfish, and other small animals when Leedsichthys blows the water back out. Many whales eat this way back in your time.

You know Leedsichthys will eventually become extinct because the animal doesn't exist in your time. The reason is possibly because seas become lower and smaller. Smaller seas will mean less food for the giant fish to eat.

**Koolasuchus—Slimy Giant**

Hit the fast-forward button in your time machine, *skipping* ahead between 40 million and 60 million years further into the Mesozoic

动物留在口腔里。在那个年代，许多鲸鱼就是这样捕食的。

你知道利兹鱼必将灭绝，因为今天已经没有这个物种了。而利兹鱼灭绝的原因可能是海域缩小、海面变浅，这就意味着这种大鱼的食物大量减少了。

酷拉龙——黏滑的巨型动物

按一下时光机的快进按钮，跳到四千万年到六千万年后，直接进入中生代。看到那个头部又宽又平、身体黏滑的娃娃鱼了吗？这就是

---

screen  *n.*  粗筛子                                   skip  *v.*  快速进入

◆ PREHISTORIC GIANTS

Era. See that slimy giant salamander with the really wide, flat head? That's Koolasuchus , an enormous amphibian, about 17 feet (5 m) long, that lives in swampy forests 137 million to 112 million years ago. Its big head holds more than 100 long teeth, which it uses to capture fish, crabs, turtles, and other prey.

Koolasuchus has eyes on top of its head. This allows it to bury itself in muddy water while keeping watch for *prey*. *Crocodiles* hunt in the same way.

Koolasuchus and other giant amphibians will disappear. A change in climate will cause them to become extinct. The change in climate will cause their swampy habitat to become less common.

酷拉龙———一种长约17英尺（5米），居住在一亿三千七百万年至一亿一千二百万年前沼泽森林里的巨型两栖动物。它大大的头里有100颗长牙，用来捕鱼、蟹、乌龟和其他猎物。

酷拉龙的眼睛长在头顶，便于它在等待猎物时藏在泥水中，鳄鱼也是这样捕食。

酷拉龙和其他巨型两栖动物也将绝迹，因为气候的变化使它们赖以生存的沼泽地越来越少。

prey  *n.*  猎物                              crocodile  *n.*  鳄鱼

**WORLD MYSTERIES**

### Giant Reptiles

During the Mesozoic, while dinosaurs walk the Earth, other giant reptiles swim in the ocean. They are just as gigantic as some dinosaurs. And just as deadly.

### Cymbospondylus—Fishlike Reptile

Cymbospondylus belongs to a group of fish like *marine* reptiles called ichthyosaurs. It lives 240 million to 210 million years ago, when it is one of the largest animals in the sea, at 33 feet (10 m) long.

Cymbospondylus has a huge head with a long, pointed snout. Its jaw contains many rows of small teeth used for catching and holding fish and other animals that it hunts in deep waters.

---

巨型爬行动物

在恐龙生活的中生代，其他巨型爬行动物在海洋中游走，它们像恐龙一样巨大，一样可怕。

杯椎龙——鱼一样的爬行动物

杯椎龙属于一种类似鱼的海洋爬行动物——鱼龙。它生活在二亿四千万年至二亿一千万年前，是当时海洋中最大的动物之一，体长达33英尺（10米）。

杯椎龙头部巨大，嘴又尖又长，里面有许多排小牙，可以捕捉在深海中的鱼及其他动物。

---

marine  *adj.*  海洋的

◆ PREHISTORIC GIANTS

### Liopleurodon—Tyrannosaurus rex of the Seas

Travel forward from the time of Cymbospondylus but stay in the ocean—if you dare. The reptile Liopleurodon swims in these salty waters, with a mouth about three times larger than that of the famous dinosaur Tyrannosaurus rex. Liopleurodon can use its large, powerful jaws to kill any animal in the seas. Like a *shark* in your time, it can smell prey from a long distance away.

Part of a group of reptiles called plesiosaurs, short-necked Liopleurodon lives 160 million to 155 million years ago. It can grow up to 49 feet (15 m) long.

---

### 滑齿龙——海中之王

从杯椎龙的时代继续向前游览，但是不要离开海洋——这可是对你胆量的考验，因为爬行动物滑齿龙正在咸咸的海水中游动。它的口腔大小是著名的雷克塞斯王龙的三倍。滑齿龙能用它巨大、有力的下颌杀死海洋中的任何一种生物。它就像是今天的鲨鱼，可以嗅到很远处的猎物。

短颈滑齿龙是爬行动物蛇颈龙的一种，生活在距今一亿六千万年至一亿五千五百万年前，它的体长可达49英尺（15米）。

---

shark  *n.*  鲨鱼

## WORLD MYSTERIES

### Elasmosaurus—Long-Necked Hunter

If you go swimming between 85 million and 65 million years ago, you might not even notice Elasmosaurus , even though it grows as long as 49 feet (15 m). Most of that length is in its neck and tail. This plesiosaur's long neck has 76 backbones in it. (The neck of a person has only eight backbones.)

Elasmosaurus can keep the *bulk* of its body far away from the fish it hunts. Its long neck allows it to *sneak* up under a school of fish without the fish knowing there is a giant under them!

### Ornithocheirus—Flying Reptile

From out of the sky, a creature the size of a small airplane

---

板龙——长颈猎者

如果你在八千五百万到六千五百万年前的海中游泳，你或许根本注意不到板龙，尽管它长达49英尺（15米）。板龙的大多数长度都在它的颈部以及尾巴上，这种蛇颈龙颈部有76块骨头（人的颈部仅有8块骨头）。

板龙能使身体主干部分远离它所要捕捉的鱼，它的长颈使它能够悄悄潜入鱼群中，而鱼群却察觉不到一个巨型动物已悄然而至！

鸟掌龙——会飞的爬行动物

在天空中，一种形似小型飞机的生物横冲过来，把它的长嘴伸进水

---

bulk  n.  主体                                      sneak  v.  偷偷地走

◆ PREHISTORIC GIANTS

swoops down, dips its long beak below the water's surface, and swallows a fish whole before flying off again. A giant bird? No. You just witnessed Ornithocheirus, a flying reptile that lives near sea coasts and lakes from 140 million to 70 million years ago. It may be the largest of the *pterosaurs*, which is a group of flying reptiles that live at the same time as the dinosaurs.

Ornithocheirus has a wingspan up to 40 feet (12.1 m) and a body about 11.5 feet (3.5 m) long. Although it is gigantic, it probably weighs only about as much as you do. That's because its bones are hollow, helping it to fly easily. Colonies of these giant flyers build nests on cliff tops.

面，吞下一条鱼后飞走了。那是一只大鸟吗？不，你刚刚看到的就是鸟掌龙，一种生活在距今一亿四千万年至七千万年前，靠近海和湖泊沿岸活动的爬行动物。它可能是和恐龙同时期会飞的、最大的飞龙目爬行动物。

鸟掌龙的翼幅达40英尺（12.1米），体长达11.5英尺（3.5米）。尽管它身形很大，但体重或许和你差不多。这是因为它的骨头是中空的，这样可以更便捷地飞行。这群大型飞龙会在悬崖顶端建巢。

pterosaurs *n.* 飞龙目

**WORLD MYSTERIES**

◆ PREHISTORIC GIANTS

## Giant Birds

You won't need *binoculars* to spot the enormous creatures called terror birds. Like today's ostriches, they are flightless, but unlike plant-eating ostriches, most (and maybe all) terror birds are *predators*.

## Gastornis—A Ton of Terror

In the forests and swamps of 56 million to 41 million years ago, you will find Gastornis, a bird about 7 feet (2.1 m) tall. It is possibly one of the top predators in North America and Europe since dinosaurs are extinct in its time.

Modern scientists are not sure what this terror bird eats, but you can see its sharp, powerful beak, which can easily *rip* the flesh and crush the bones of small animals—if it can catch them. Gastornis may weigh more than 1 ton.

---

巨型鸟类

你不必用双筒望远镜来观察巨型生物"骇鸟"。就像今天的鸵鸟一样，骇鸟不能飞翔；然而鸵鸟属于食草动物，大部分（或许全部）的骇鸟却属于肉食类动物。

戈氏鸟——一种更恐怖的鸟

在距今5600万年至4100万年的森林和沼泽地里，你会发现戈氏鸟——一种高达7英尺（2.1米）的鸟。它可能是那个时代从恐龙灭绝后在北美以及欧洲最大的肉食性动物了。

当代科学家不能确定这种骇鸟以什么为食，但是可以看到它有着尖锐、有力的鸟喙。这样，如果它捉到小动物，就可以轻而易举地用嘴撕开动物身体，并敲碎动物的骨头。戈氏鸟的体重可能会超过1吨。

---

binoculars *n.* 双筒望远镜　　　　　　　　predator *n.* 食肉动物
rip *v.* 撕开

WORLD MYSTERIES

### Phorusrhacos—Speedy and Deadly

Phorusrhacos is a terror bird that stands up to 10 feet (3 m) tall. It hunts small animals in plains and woodlands from 27 million to 2.5 million years ago, possibly catching such prey as young saber-toothed cats and small horses.

Phorusrhacos can move much faster than Gastornis because it doesn't weigh as much as that earlier terror bird. Phorusrhacos may be able to *run after* its prey at 43 miles (69 km) per hour, faster than a car usually travels down a city street.

### Giant Mammals

After the extinction of the giant reptiles, giant mammals began to

---

恐鹤——瞬间致命

恐鹤是一种立身长达10英尺（3米）的骇鸟。它生活在二千七百万到二百五十万年前，在平原以及林原捕食长有上犬齿的猫类以及小马等猎物。

恐鹤要比戈氏鸟飞得快得多，因为它没有戈氏鸟那么重。恐鹤能够追逐一个以每小时43英里（69千米）速度奔跑的猎物，这比一辆在城市街道常速行驶的汽车还要快。

④巨型哺乳动物

继巨型爬行动物绝迹后，巨型哺乳动物开始统治这个世界。许多科学

---

run after  追逐

◆ PREHISTORIC GIANTS

rule the world. Many scientists believe terror birds went extinct later in the Cenozoic era because mammals were better hunters—they ate all the food! But the giant mammals you are about to meet are *herbivores*, meaning they eat only plants, so don't be afraid to get close.

### Indricotherium—Dino-Sized Rhino

Climb a tree to get a good look at Indricotherium, a relative of today's rhinoceros. This giant mammal uses its long neck, like a giraffe, to eat leaves and *branches* at the tops of trees.

---

家认为骇鸟在新生代后期绝迹，因为哺乳动物是捕猎能手，它们基本上什么都吃！然而你将要见到的哺乳动物是食草类的，它们只吃植物，所以你可以放心地靠近它们。

⑤灵兽——体型可怕的犀牛

爬到树上仔细观看灵兽，会觉得它有点像今天的犀牛。这种巨型哺乳动物有着长颈鹿一样的脖子，可以吃到树顶的树枝和树叶。

---

herbivore  *n.*  食草动物                branch  *n.*  树枝

**WORLD MYSTERIES**

Living from 30 million to 25 million years ago, Indricotherium is at least 15 feet (4.5 m) tall— bigger than a one-story house—and it weighs 16 tons (15 metric tons). The big body of Indricotherium allows it to *store* a great amount of fat and water. This helps the big animal survive long hot and dry seasons.

**Gigantopithecus—The Real King Kong**

King Kong was a big ape in a movie, but Gigantopithecus is a real giant ape that lives from about 8 million to 100,000 years ago. Some males stand 10 feet (3 m) tall on their hind legs and weigh

---

灵兽生活在三千万年到二千五百万年前，其身高至少达15英尺（4.5米），比一座平房还要高大。它重达16吨（15公吨）。灵兽巨大的身体内能够贮存大量的脂肪和水，所以这种大型动物能够在长期干燥、酷热的环境中生存。

巨猿——真正的金刚

金刚是出现在电影里的大类人猿，然而巨猿是真正生活在八百万年到十万年前的巨型猿类。有些雄性巨猿后腿站立时身高可达10英尺（3

---

store v. 贮存

◆ PREHISTORIC GIANTS

more than 1,000 pounds (454 kilograms). You can tell which ones are females. They are half this size.

Gigantopithecus is a *gentle* giant. It eats bamboo, fruit, seeds, and other plant food in tropical *rainforests* in Asia.

While you're here, you might even spot an early type of human called Homo erectus, who is living at the same time and in the same places as Gigantopithecus. These humans may end up using so much bamboo for food and to make tools that not enough will be left for Gigantopithecus to eat. This is one possible reason why Gigantopithecus will become extinct.

---

米），重达1000磅（454公斤）。雌性巨猿很容易分辨，因为它们身材仅有雄性的一半。

巨猿是一种温和的巨型动物。它以亚洲热带雨林的竹子、水果、种子以及其他植物为食。

走在这里，你甚至会看到一种被称作直立人的早期人类。他们和巨猿生活在同一时段、同一地点。这些人类以竹子为食，用竹子制作工具，使得巨猿没有足够的竹子可吃，这可能是巨猿绝迹的原因之一。

---

gentle *adj.* 温和的                              rainforest *n.* 雨林

**WORLD MYSTERIES**

### Mammuthus—Woolly Mammoth and Its Relatives

Time to move forward again to between 4 million and 10,000 years ago, during the last ice age, to catch a *glimpse* of a woolly mammoth, a species of Mammuthus. Keep your eyes peeled for a creature that looks like a huge hairy elephant, with long curved *tusks*. There it is, using its tusks to clear paths through snow, probably searching for plant food. The woolly mammoth stands almost 12 feet (3.6 m) tall, but another Mammuthus species can grow as tall as 14 feet (4.3 m).

Early humans hunt mammoths and paint pictures of them, which

---

猛犸象属——猛犸象及其亲属

时间再一次快进到四百万年和一万年前的上一次冰河世纪，在这里可以看一下猛犸象（猛犸象属的一种）。猛犸象是一种巨型毛象，长着弯弯的长牙，你不妨非常专心地观察一番。猛犸象用长牙在雪地上清出道路，它们也许是在觅食植物。猛犸象几乎有12英尺（3.6米）高，还有另一种猛犸象身高可达14英尺（4.3米）。

早期人类捕猎猛犸象，并且在它们身上绘画，类似的图画在今日欧洲

---

glimpse n. 一瞥      tusk n. （象的）长牙

◆ PREHISTORIC GIANTS

can still be seen on cave walls in modern Europe. Mammoths will become extinct at the end of the ice age, when the weather becomes too warm for them.

Megatherium—Giant Ground Sloth

Don't *take off* your winter coat yet. Another huge mammal that lives during the last ice age is Megatherium, a giant ground sloth. It lives about 2 million to 8,000 years ago and is almost 20 feet (6 m) long.

Megatherium *is related to* the much smaller tree sloths that live in South America today. The one you're watching is standing on its hind legs, using its tail for balance, which shouldn't surprise you. Fossil footprints found in your time showed that it could stand and even walk upright.

---

洞穴的穴壁上仍然能够看到。此次冰河世纪末期，猛犸象由于无法适应变暖的气候而逐渐消亡。

巨型地懒——巨型地面树懒

现在还不要褪去冬装。另一种居住在上次冰河世纪的巨型哺乳动物是巨型地懒（一种巨型地面树懒）。它居住在二百万到八千年前，身长可达20英尺（6米）。

巨型地懒和现在南美洲的小树懒属于同一家族。你眼前的大树懒正在用后腿站立，用尾巴保持平衡，这应该没什么奇怪的，因为今天发现的化石脚印表明，它能够站立甚至可以直立行走。

---

take off  脱下　　　　　　　　　　　be related to  与……有联系

## WORLD MYSTERIES

And speaking of your time, you should probably be getting back...

### A World Without Giants?

Isn't it amazing to think that giants such as the ones in this book once walked on Earth and swam in the ocean? It's too bad we can't see these huge creatures today.

However, you don't have to get in a time machine to see very large animals. Blue whales, great white sharks, giant squids, *grizzly* bears, elephants, giraffes, ostriches, *condors*, and *anacondas* are some of the large animals that share the planet with us today.

---

说到"今天",也是该回到今天的时候了……
没有巨型动物的世界会怎样?
想想这本书中提到的巨型动物曾在地上走过或在水中游过,感觉很神奇吧?遗憾的是我们再也不能亲眼看到这些巨型动物了。
然而,并不一定要搭乘时空机才能看到巨型动物。蓝鲸、大白鲨、巨型乌贼、灰熊、大象、长颈鹿、鸵鸟、秃鹰和水蟒都是地球上的巨型动

---

grizzly *adj.* 灰白的
anaconda *n.* 蟒蛇

candor *n.* 秃鹫

◆ PREHISTORIC GIANTS

Unfortunately, many of these animals are *threatened* with extinction because their populations are so small. It's important to protect these animals, mainly by preserving their habitats. That way, we can be sure that we'll never live in a world without giants.

物。不幸的是，许多物种的数量正日趋减少，濒临灭绝。保护好这些物种意义重大，尤其要保护好它们的栖息之地。只有这样，我们才能与巨型动物共同生活在这个地球上。

threaten *v.* 威胁